Texas Fish & Game®

presents

Flounder FEVER

By Chester Moore

OTHER TITLES PUBLISHED BY
TEXAS FISH & GAME PUBLISHING CO., LLC

BOOKS:

Saltwater Strategies®: Where, When & How to Wadefish Texas
by Bink Grimes

*Freshwater Strategies®: A Practical Approach
to Texas Freshwater Fishing*
by Doug Pike

Saltwater Strategies®: Texas Reds
by Chester Moore, Jr.

Saltwater Strategies®: Texas Trout Tactics
by Chester Moore, Jr.

*Saltwater Strategies®: Pat Murray's No-Nonsense
Guide to Coastal Fishing*
by Pat Murray

Texas Saltwater Classics: Fly Patterns for the Texas Coast
by Greg Berlocher

Doreen's 24 Hour Eat Gas Now Café
by Reavis Z. Wortham

PERIODICALS:

Texas Fish & Game Magazine (12x/year)
Texas Lakes & Bays Atlas (annual)

for information, contact us at:
1-800-750-4678
www.fishgame.com

Texas Fish & Game Publishing Co., LLC
1745 Greens Road • Houston, Texas 77032
1-800-750-4678 • Fax: 713-227-3002

Texas Fish & Game®

presents

Flounder
FEVER

By Chester Moore

**TEXAS FISH & GAME
PUBLISHING CO., L.L.C.**

1745 Greens Road • Houston, Texas 77032
1-800-750-4678
www.fishgame.com

Published by
Texas Fish & Game
Publishing Co., L.L.C.
1745 Greens Road
Houston Texas 77032
Phone: 281-227-3001 Fax: 281-227-3002
Website: www.fishgame.com

First Edition

Foreword by Don Zaidle

All photos by Chester Moore unless otherwise credited.

Layout design by Wendy Kipfmiller

Production by Doug Berry

Edited by Don Zaidle.

ISBN: 0-929980-18-2

This book is dedicated to my parents for their undying support of everything that I do. Also, to Lisa for being there for me no matter how driven I get and for her endless love. And also to Hallie for always making me smile and letting me know someone else is as nutty (in a good way) as I am

Contents

foreword

I shall never forget my first face-to-face meeting with Chester Moore. He, a few other *Texas Fish & Game* magazine staffers, and I were hunting teal and alligators one September with Central Flyway Outfitters near Winnie, Texas, a few miles from the Anahuac National Wildlife Refuge.

Chester and a guide named Jessie went trolling for gators in a "mud boat" (so named because it can literally navigate mud) in a shallow backwater of a bayou. The rest of the county and I knew something was up when Chester started whooping like a wild Indian.

Out on the water, Chester stood on the tiny bow of the mud boat, reared back against the resistance at the other end of his bowfishing line. Resistance? Make that Peterbilt road tractor-class power. Whatever Chester had arrowed was towing the heavy boat fast enough to leave a respectable wake. They disappeared behind a tangle of trees and marsh grass. Things got spookily quiet for a bit, then shouts, loud splashing, and the report of a .357 Magnum shattered the silence. A few minutes later, the mud boat started up, and here came Chester and company with his prize: the largest alligator gar I have ever seen.

As I recall, the fish measured more than 7 feet and weighed close to 275 pounds. Chester was so jazzed he couldn't think straight. I asked what his wife, Lisa, would think about him dragging such a monster home. He looked at me bewildered for several seconds, then blurted, "Oh, *Lisa!*"

Later, I was setting up photos of Chester with the prehistoric giant. In one of the setups, Chester had pulled the gar up in a face-to-face pose. It struck me how much he and that gar resembled in profile. I labeled him "Garface" on the spot.

If Chester is anywhere in sight, you can count on adventure being somewhere mighty close. Not that he creates adventure, he simply has a knack for finding it. The reason, I think, is because he is so passionate about hunting, fishing, and nature in general.

Actually, Chester is passionate about everything he does, and goes "whole hog" for whatever pie he sticks his fingers into. His life is a study in superlatives. He was not content with being an amateur naturalist, so he earned a degree in zoology. He hunts for whatever moves and is legal, fishes for the exotic and mundane with equal enthusiasm, pushes envelopes, chases horizons, and challenges the status quo. He is equally at home sitting on a jetty catching sheepshead with a cane pole, or hunting bighorns in the high country with celebrities. He is at once a traditionalist and a renaissance man, and someone you feel privileged to call "friend."

As you will learn within these pages, Chester's passion and enthusiasm extends to the "lowly" southern flounder. Nonetheless, if Chester were a fish, I doubt it would be a flounder; that's too sedentary. He would be a shark or kingfish or barracuda...or maybe an alligator gar; he has the face for it.

—*Don Zaidle*
Managing Editor
Texas Fish & Game magazine

Introduction

Flounder fishing has always inspired me. Growing up, my father, Chester Moore, Sr., taught me to fish for many species, ranging from speckled trout to alligator garfish, but flounder always held a special appeal. Looking back, it was a combination of things that drew me to pursue flounder so doggedly throughout my life. The capper was having a monstrous flounder break off right at the boat when I was nine or ten years old, but there was just something about flatfish that was different from the other fish. Sure, they looked different, and with me, that was probably a factor. I have always been a fan of the strange and unusual in nature—and flounder are weird.

These fish are born with an eye on each side like other fishes, and then after a few months, one eye migrates to the other side. Then they fish spend their life camouflaged on the bottom waiting for food to swim by. Add some nuclear testing, and you have a candidate for a new villain in Japan's Godzilla franchise. I can see it now: "Godzilla vs. the Flounder from Hell—Battle in the Gulf of Mexico."

Seriously, tracing my love for flounder brings back many warm memories of fishing with family and friends and catching something I knew even at an early age was special to many people. Later on, I learned that the fish has a "cult following," but at the time, I thought everybody held flounder in high regard.

One of my favorite flounder fishing memories is when my father, my lifelong friend Chris Villadsen, and I fished the Louisiana shoreline of Sabine Lake with mud minnows. Dad heard the flounder were biting, so we stocked up on mud minnows and set out for a day of fishing. We brought home 15 flounder, which we did not measure because, at the time, that was not an issue, but they were all big. I still have a very cloudy picture of this catch, and next to the flounder is a big redfish we caught. One of the flounder was almost as big as the redfish, which I dare say would today require a trophy tag in Texas waters. That was the first time I saw so many big flounder caught in one sitting, and that one trip taught me a lot about what to look for in a flounder fishing location.

To this day, I frequent that spot. In fact, I fished there just a few hours before sitting down to write this Introduction, and it still holds plenty of flounder.

Another memory that sticks in my mind is my father and me walking out into some marsh to seek redfish, and me seeing a huge flounder (at least to my young eyes) buried in the mud right along the shoreline. I caught its outline while watching mud minnows, which I assume the flatfish was about to engulf. I ran over to grab a landing net to try to scoop up the thing, but the flounder was not buying it. The big, beautiful fish disappeared in a flurry of mud, and I stood fascinated by what I had seen.

I have always been one of those people entranced by predator-prey relations. Back then, I watched every Jacques Cousteau and *Wild Kingdom* program that came on TV. Nowadays, I get in shark cages and watch great white sharks feed from point-blank range. I love the whole survival of the fittest thing in nature.

Watching that flounder blend into the mud and wait for the mud minnows to come by was a valuable lesson for me. I did not consciously recognize it then, but I believe that one encounter taught me more about flounder than just about anything else did.

In reading this book, you will realize the one theme that permeates every chapter is that flounder are lazy, opportunistic fish. Forget finding them aggressively feeding under the birds (although I have caught a flounder that way) or smacking topwater plugs on a regular basis. These fish simply lie on the bottom and rely on camouflage and the tides for survival.

Take a minute to think about popular flounder fishing areas in your region and you will probably think of two or three spots that people always fish. There are such spots for speckled trout and redfish, but they are not so concrete. Specks and reds might be on the main body of a bay feeding one day, and the same schools might be two miles away the next. That is not going to happen with flounder for the most part. These fish have their traditional places to inhabit, and they stay there until it is time to migrate in and out of bay systems.

I think the key word here is "tradition." I am a big fan of fishing traditions, and watching an elderly man wearing white shrimping boots in his aluminum boat tied off to a bridge all day catching flounder is something I saw in my youth, and still see to this day. Flounder fishing techniques are passed on from generation to generation in a genuine passionate way, and that is something sorely lacking in the fishing community these days.

While I am a fan of traditions, I am certainly all for exploration, and that is what this book represents: tradition and exploration. For every old flounder secret revealed, there is something new I or someone I know discovered. This book represents my deep passion for flounder fishing tradition and breaking new ground in this exciting fishery.

I have included tips and tactics that will likely anger some traditionalists who do not want their secrets revealed, but I believe in sharing information. This book contains just about everything I know or have heard regarding flounder fishing. My first flounder book, *Flounder Fundamentals*, came out nearly four years ago, and while I am proud of that work, this one buries it in terms of information on putting flounder in your ice chest. I have simply learned that much more since the last go-round, and look forward to sharing it with all of you diehard flounder fishing fanatics.

Chapter One

A flounder's life

Imagine getting to lie around the pool concealed from everyone, watching the world go by, and having fresh fish delivered to you any time you want it. Then once a year, you head out toward the Gulf to mate and come back to the coast in the spring.

Sounds like a good life to me—well, except for the mating only once a year thing.

That is essentially the life of the flounder. They lie camouflaged on the bottom, the tides bring fish to them, and then make one big trip to mate once a year. Flounder, compared to other coastal fish, really have it easy. They are, indeed, a unique species among sport fishes found along the coast of the Gulf of Mexico, with virtually everything about them being different.

Paralichthys lethostigma, the southern flounder, is the largest of more than 25 species of flatfishes found in Gulf coastal waters, and it is the subspecies covered in this book. Anglers occasionally catch other varieties, but dockside harvest surveys show that southern flounder

1

make up 95 percent of the flatfish catch in the Gulf.

Southern flounder occur from the Carolinas all the way into Mexico. They are most common west of the Mississippi River, and that is where recreational anglers pursue them most doggedly.

All flatfishes, including the southern flounder, are lateral and

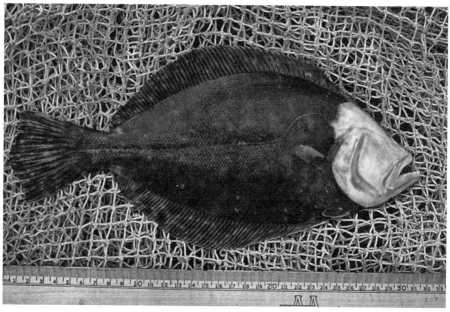

Southern flounder—notice eyes are on the left side (facing down).

spend most of their lives on the bottom, where they swim on their sides and lie in ambush for unsuspecting baitfishes. In the case of the southern flounder, the left side is always the "up" side, while in other species, the opposite is true.

The flounder is tailor made for life on the bottom. When the fish first hatch, they have eyes on each side like other fishes, but eventually those eyes migrate to one side. Both eyes in adults are on the "up" side of the head, and the coloration of the upper side of the body varies greatly to match the surrounding environment. The down side of all flounder is solid white.

Anglers often catch flounder that look almost coal black, but they spot up when held. That is the flounder's attempt to match its new surroundings. (No one ever said they were intelligent creatures, just adaptable.) Flounder can change their colors more than most anglers realize. I once kept several flounder in a 400-gallon aquarium I built in

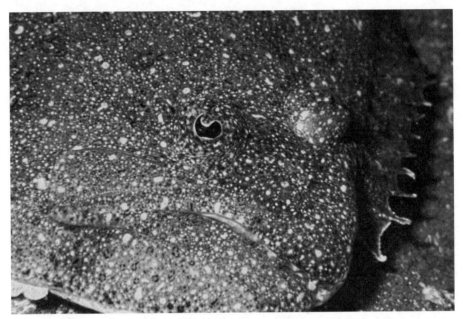

Dusky flounder—notice eyes are right side up.

my workshop for fish behavior study. The sand in the aquarium was finely sifted white sand. The flounder in this tank turned a very, very light shade of gray, and their normally white spots were almost a luminescent white. It was very interesting to see. Later, in another aquarium, I kept some flounder on black gravel and they turned a very dark brown, almost black. Being able to adjust their colors to fit surroundings is an adaptation that allows them to hunt by ambush very effectively, and make a living by lying around spots other fishes pass by.

Another unique characteristic is the absence of an air bladder, which keeps most fish species buoyant. This allows the flounder to hold tightly to the bottom where it spends most of its time.

There is some debate over the life history of these fish, but TPWD fisheries biologists give a good explanation in a publication called *The Southern Flounder in Texas*:

> Adult southern flounder leave the bays during the fall for spawning in the Gulf of Mexico. They spawn for the first time when two years old at depths of 50 to 100 feet. The eggs are buoyant. Females become sexually mature at two years of age in Texas waters. The youngest mature female southern flounder in northern Florida was four years old according to scientists there. Of the mature females collected in August, eight percent of the four year-olds, five percent of the five year olds, and 18 percent of the six-year-olds were developing eggs.
>
> Lab technicians induced southern flounders in Texas to spawn in the laboratory in an experiment conducted by the University of Texas in 1977. About three weeks before spawning took place, males began following females in the tanks. The first spawning was on December 21. Spawning was at midday, when females swam to the surface and released eggs that attending males immediately fertilized. This evidence shows that females might induce the fall migrations.
>
> After hatching, the larval fish swim in an upright position and the eyes are located on opposite sides of the head. As the young fish grows, the right eye begins to "migrate" to the left side of the head. When body

length reaches one-half inch or so, the eye migration is complete and the fish assumes its left-side-up position for life.

The young fish enter the bays during late winter and early spring. At this time, they are about one-half inch in length and seek shallow grassy areas near the Gulf passes. As growth continues, some will move farther into bays. Some will enter coastal rivers and bayous.

Southern flounder postlarvae show up all along the Gulf of Mexico coast during winter and early spring. According to studies in Aransas Bay, Texas, the peak movement of postlarvae flounders into estuaries is in February, when water temperatures are still low.

Juveniles 50 to 100 mm were caught on the seaward beaches of islands in Louisiana in April, and fish 34 to 57 mm long showed up in areas of the Mobile Delta during December and from February to April.

Near the mouth of the Mississippi River, adults and juveniles appeared during summer in addition to a few adults taken in winter near Galveston Island, Texas.

Juvenile flounder feed mainly on crustaceans, but as they grow, fish become more important in their diet. Adult flounder enter shallow water at night where they lie, often partially buried, and wait for prey. Empty depressions where flounder have lain are labeled as "beds."

According to a Texas A&M University report, scientists know little about southern flounder growth rates:

It has been determined that southern flounder females grow approximately three times faster than males. As with other flatfish, the sex of the fish is not determined until after metamorphosis; the precise time is not known for southern flounder. In Japanese flounder, the sex of the fish can be influenced by temperature.

The optimum temperature for producing the highest percentage of females is approximately 70 degrees. Temperatures significantly higher or lower than that likely will result in a higher percentage of males in the overall population. In captive breeding programs in Japan, high stocking densities may also shift the population towards males.

Southern flounder are cannibalistic and feed aggressively. This aggressive behavior leads to uneven growth rates, so they must be graded often to increase survival in captivity.

Small flounder grow rapidly and may reach 12 inches in length by the end of their first year. Males seldom exceed 12 inches, but females grow larger than males and often reach a length of 25 inches. Most flounder caught by anglers are females between 12 and 16 inches long, weighing from 1 to 1-1/2 pounds.

This does not mean flounder cannot get huge. The Texas state record is a 13-pounder caught by H. Endicott of Groves at Sabine Lake in 1976. The world record, 20 lbs., 9 oz., was caught caught by Larenza

Larenza Mungin with his world record southern flounder.

Mungin while pier fishing in Florida in 1983, and there have been reports of a number of truly monstrous flounder caught throughout the years. A.C. Becker caught a 17-pounder in a shrimp trawl in the mouth

Texas Elite Angler Ken Thyssen with his qualifying Southern flounder.

of Double Bayou near Anahuac, Texas, in 1948. Over the years, I have talked with several shrimpers who have decked flounder they thought were bigger than the state record. I do not doubt these stories for a second.

Trey Ganem of Victoria, Texas, once gave me a picture of a flounder he gigged near Port Aransas. The fish measured 33 inches, and from the picture, it looked every bit that large. Ganem did not weigh the fish, but I can tell you it was a true beast.

To attain such size, a flounder would have to be very old and a supreme predator—which is exactly what flounder are.

In the excellent book, *Flounder: How, When & Where*, written by the late, great Galveston Daily News Outdoors Editor A.C. Becker, the author gives what I feel is a perfect explanation of the attraction of flounder: "It's a challenge to catch and a gourmet's delight!" I mention this because there simply is no better explanation of why I pursue these fish. Becker said it best, so there is no reason to try to improve on it.

Flounder do not put up impressive jumping displays like a tarpon, nor do they make brutal, determined runs like a redfish, but they are certainly a challenge to catch. I defy anyone to find a fish that tastes better than flounder; there are not any.

They do not chase and corral schools of baitfishes like speckled trout, redfish, mackerel, and sharks do. Flounder simply lie on the bottom and wait for the prey to come to them. Sometimes it is possible to encounter flounder chasing baitfishes on a shallow flat or point, but for the most part, flounder stay on the bottom, wait for a prey item to come by, attack it, and settle back down on the bottom. It is a very effective way of making a living.

Understanding this dynamic is the key to catching these delectable, challenging fish. To become a genuine flatfish expert, you have to forget what you know about reds and specks. It is an entirely different world—one that is easy to obsess about.

SCIENTISTS PRODUCING FEMALE ONLY FLOUNDER

Sea Grant researchers at North Carolina State University are turning up the heat on southern flounder to produce all-female cultured stocks. The controlled-breeding method relies on water temperature manipulation, not on genetic engineering, during the flounder's early development.

From a pure science standpoint, the research results are

important since most temperature-dependent sex determination has been documented in reptiles, such as some turtles and lizards, and all crocodilians.

"From an economic standpoint, that is significant," said Russell Borski, a zoology professor and member of the flounder research "dream team."

The production of all-female stock pushes the southern flounder up a notch as a candidate for aquaculture in North Carolina. Studies show that female flounder grow two to three times the size of male flounder within two years, a reasonable grow-out period for aquaculture operations. Given the high consumer demand and high world-market value for flounder, the ability to produce larger fish in a short period of time could add up to handsome investment returns.

The production of farm-raised finfish, such as hybrid striped bass, tilapia, and trout, is expanding in North Carolina, according to state Department of Agriculture and Consumer Services figures. However, there are no southern flounder-farming operations that rear fish from egg to market-size anywhere in the U.S.

Maybe these techniques can aid ailing flounder populations in the wild.

Chapter Two

Choosing flounder gear

Flounder do not require a lot of fancy gear to catch. In fact, I know some land-bound anglers who use only a homemade cane pole to consistently catch good stringers of flatfish. Cane poles are far from ideal and very limiting, but it goes to show you don't have to make six figures a year to afford flounder tackle. One of my favorite things about flounder is that you can catch them from the bank, and there hasn't been an elitist slant yet put to pursuing them. Part of that is because of the simplicity of the gear, although some anglers seem to want a more grandiose explanation. Fishermen at my seminars ask dozens of questions about how to gear up, and some seemed quite disappointed when I tell them there is not much to it. However, I do believe choosing the "right" gear is crucial, so read on.

Rods and Reels

A good flounder rod is stiff. It is imperative that a rod be limber enough to work an artificial lure if you so choose, but it should still be as stiff as practicable. Along the Texas and Louisiana coasts, casting combos are the most popular. They are durable, can handle big fish, and cast a long ways. In flounder fishing, the only useful characteristic of those three is durability. You do not necessarily need a rod that can handle a big fish (flounder don't get very big) and you should not make long casts (it messes up hookset and the action of many artificial baits).

Unless I am fishing for trophy flounder in deep water, I never use casting equipment. I always use spinning gear—which we will get into shortly—but since many anglers like casting equipment, here is the rundown.

The average medium-heavy action popping rod is adequate for flounder. They have a stiff enough backbone to make a forceful hookset, and the action allows for using artificial lures. There are many, many good ones on the market. All-Star, Castaway, Berkley, Falcon, and Shakespeare all make top-notch stuff. The yellow Eagle Claw popping rods available at most Academy stores are good and very affordable.

There are just as many quality casting reels on the market. I am partial to the Abu Garcia Ambassadeur and the Quantum Iron series, but have equally good things to say about Daiwa, Browning, Pinnacle, Penn, and others. Do not worry about finding a reel that holds a whole bunch of line because flounder don't make long runs most of the time.

Spinning gear is much more effective for flounder fishing, in my opinion. It is easy to flip into cover like stands of roseau cane and little pockets of jetties. It also allows an artificial bait to sink more naturally, thus enhancing the chances of a hookup. My personal favorite flounder setup is an old 6-1/2-foot Shakespeare rod that I cut down to 5 feet, 10 inches, that is rigged with an Abu Garcia Suveran spinning reel. The Suveran is a smooth caster with a unique frontal drag system.

The essence of this setup is the rod. Flounder have very bony mouths and are hard to put a hook into. An extra stiff rod enhances forceful hookset into a fish. My friends often refer to my flounder setup as a "pool cue," but they are not laughing when I out-fish them and their limber little rods by two to one.

It is worth mentioning that for youngsters or beginners some of the spin-cast combos like the Zebco 808 are actually pretty good for flounder fishing. In fact, one fishing guide I know keeps several of them in his arsenal for anglers who are not confident with casting or spinning gear.

While it is not necessary to have expensive tackle to flounder fish, you do get what you pay for. Some low-end products will last a long time, but going the extra mile and buying a couple of nice flounder setups will save money in the long run. If taken care of most, $250-300 combos will last most of a lifetime.

Pool cue rig

CHOOSING THE RIGHT LINE

There are so many brands, sizes, colors, and varieties of fishing lines today, selecting one it can be truly mind-boggling. Some of these

Fishing roseau cane

are good for all-around fishing while others are excellent for very specific applications.

Most so-called "super lines' are actually braids lines, and some fusion lines are hard to categorize, so I'll refer all of them as "super-lines." In my opinion, certain super lines are the most effective. They have virtually no stretch, which enhances hookset into bony flounder mouths. Another advantage is power, which comes in handy when you are fishing the surf and hook into a wayward blacktip shark or tarpon.

Some super lines are the diameter of 6-pound-test traditional monofilament, but rated 20-pound-test, providing castability and strength in a single package. That is pretty neat stuff, if you ask me.

Since about 1996, all of my flounder reels are spooled with some kind of super line, especially the spinning reels. My personal favorite is Berkley Fireline, but Spiderwire, Spider Fusion, Power Pro, and Tough Line are all worth a try.

Something to keep in mind is that many super lines come in greenish colors. On my home water, Sabine Lake, most fish will hardly look at a bait fished on a green line; they are line-shy for some reason. When I use smoke-colored Fireline, I get bites. While fishing with my cousin, Frank Moore, in one of the hottest flounder spots in existence, he out-fished me two to one using smoke-colored Fireline. At the time, I was using a new green color and could hardly get a bite. When we switched rods, the roles reversed and he couldn't get a bite. Try to match the line color to the water you are fishing. The water on Sabine Lake is always brown, so the smoke matches up better than green.

There is a serious drawback to super lines: backlash. If you get a backlash with braided or fusion line, forget about untangling it. Get out the knife and start cutting. I use braided line on spinning reels most of the time, so I do not have much of a problem, but friends who use it are converting to anti-backlash reels. Capt. Terry Shaunessy of the Hackberry Rod & Gun Club said he puts a backing of monofilament on his bait-casting spools and then weaves in the braided line. He said this cuts down on backlash problems in a big way.

Some might disagree that fluorocarbon line does not belong in the "super line" category, but I put it there anyway. It has some super properties. Fluorocarbon line has been commonly used for years, especially in clear water areas like South Florida and by fly-fishermen who pursue wary trout in clear northern streams. This stuff is nearly invisible in the water. It gets its name from a chemical called, well, fluorocarbon. It has close to the same light refraction qualities as water, which makes it disappear below the surface.

Recently, I have used a fluorocarbon-coated line called P-Line with great success. It has served well in some tough situations.

I have always said a fishing line that can stand up to offshore species caught around oil rigs can stand up anywhere. Offshore species fight harder and grow larger than their inshore counterparts, and barnacle-encrusted oil rig pilings makes angling even more challenging.

For a test I wrote up in *Texas Fish & Game* magazine, I took out some of the P-Line CXX X-TRA Strong fishing line to the oil rigs out of Galveston. I fished with the original P-Line, a super strong monofilament, in Venezuela in December 1999 and found it great for yanking big peacock bass out of the brushy, flooded rainforest around Lake Guri. I wanted to see if the CXX X-TRA Strong would yield the same results in the Gulf. It did.

My fishing partner, Bill Killian, and I were free-lining live shrimp around some platforms and catching big sheepshead and southern pompano. The fish held tight to the platform legs, so we had to tighten down our drags and pull the fish away before they hit the sharp barnacles. We found no problem with cranking down the drag to nearly nothing on the 17-pound-test, and pulling the hard-fighting fish into the boat. In fact, one of the pompano brushed the line against the platform legs, but it did not break, which says a lot for its abrasion resistance.

When fishing for smaller species, anglers walk a fine line with the lines they use—no pun intended. Braided lines give better sensitivity than any mono, but the lack of stretch can cause problems in deep water. Regular mono stretches too much and does not have the abrasion resistance. P-Line is an in-between for anglers who do not know which way to go. Its stealth qualities help tremendously. In the situation described earlier, I discovered that the normally line shy pompano took our baits with abandon, I believe it was because we were using fluorocarbon P-Line.

There is nothing wrong with using monofilament. Mono manufacturing techniques have improved dramatically over the last few years. Stren Sensor and Berkley Big Game come to mind as excellent choices. These have very low stretch properties and little line memory.

Another excellent line is Excalibur. This stuff has incredible abrasion resistance, which is a big plus in flounder fishing. While using 14-pound Excalibur, I hooked a Spanish mackerel at an oil platform in the Gulf of Mexico. The fish wrapped itself around one of the barnacle-encrusted pilings but it did not cut the line. Impressive.

When considering a specific brand of monofilament for flounder fishing, always keep in mind stretch and abrasion resistance. Something else to keep in mind is color. Normally I would stick with something clear, but the Triple Fish line, which is camouflage, is intriguing. I have used it on a couple of trips to the short rigs out of Sabine Pass and found it an excellent choice. I did not catch any more or less fish using it, so I call that a success.

There is no reason to go in-depth about monofilament line, as most of the ones on the market are of great quality and will get the job done. Just keep in mind that most of the time you want to use as small a diameter of line as you can get away with for flounder fishing, but still retain strength. Going ultra light is crazy unless you want the thrill of playing a fish, but if you want to actually land it, set your drag and use something that can handle most any fish. Lines in the 12- or 14-pound class can handle anything out there, as long as you have your drag set properly. In most applications, there is no use going higher for flounder. That is what super lines are for.

Chapter
Three

Fly-fishing, spearing, and other flounder strategies

I caught my first flounder on a fly rod a couple of years ago. I am not a big fly-fisherman, but do find battling fish on a fly rod exciting. The fish I caught was about 2 pounds and it reminded me of something fly-fishing expert Phil Shook of Houston once told me. He said the finesse that goes along with fly-fishing goes hand in hand with catching flounder.

Very few anglers pursue flounder with a fly rod, but there are many opportunities along the Gulf Coast. I have not caught many flounder on a fly rod, but plan on pursuing them doggedly on fly gear in the future.

I learned to fly-fish on my own, but recommend that first-timers take lessons from an expert. It is not difficult stuff to learn, but there are many little things that an expert can teach you in days or even minutes that could otherwise take years to learn.

A 6- to 8-weight rod with matching weight-forward fly line is probably the best bet. I have talked with several fishermen who said any line would work, but several recommended weight-forward line because of good experiences with it.

Some novices might do best to fish with a 9-foot, 9-weight fly rod, which might be overgunning some of the smaller flounder that can be expected to inhale a fly, but it offers easier castability and greater range. On the Gulf Coast, that comes in handy with the strong winds that prevail much of the year. If a person cannot make good casts, he cannot catch fish. It is that simple.

Purchasing fly-fishing gear is another scenario where you get what you pay for. If you plan on trying this sport, you might want to get an inexpensive saltwater combo. If you are really into it, more expensive gear is required.

Nowadays, anglers have a huge variety of flies to choose from, many of which are as effective as they are colorful. While fly-fishing for rainbow trout in the Little Red River in Arkansas, I traded fly notes with a guide who makes his living fly-fishing. Some of the flies we use on the coast are very similar to the ones used for rainbows and browns.

Here are some of the best for flounder, which also double for specks and redfish.

CLOUSER MINNOW: Most saltwater fly-fishermen say if they had just one fly to use forever, this would be it. It is great in the shallows and in deeper water.

Clouser Minnow

DECEIVER MENHADEN: This is another popular fly and one I have fished with—a white and pink pattern tied on a 5/0 hook.

BAY ANCHOVY: There are many of good patterns of small translucent baitfishes to consider. These are great because they come in many sizes and can help you "match the hatch," which is discussed elsewhere in this book. You can get these 1/2 to 3 inches long.

Bay Anchovy

POPPERS: These are fun to fish with because they are the topwater plugs of the fly-fishing world. Enough said.

Danno's Poppin Shrimp

DEER HAIR MULLET: This is a good one for fishing in marshy areas.

LEFTY'S DECEIVER: This fly gets it name from fly-fishing legend Lefty Kreh, and produces when others will not. It is very popular among fly-fishing enthusiasts, particularly in Florida.

Lefty's Deceiver

CHUMMING

Chumming is not a common technique in flounder fishing, or anywhere in bay fishing, for that matter, but some anglers do it. The late Johnny Fontenot of Galveston used to chum with a bag of mashed up shrimp and crab at the Galveston jetties. He once told me it got the attention of flounder bedded up in the crevices of the jetties. He would sink a lingerie bag filled with chum down to the bottom and cast a live mud minnow a few feet in front of it. He never moved his bait, but just let the fish come to it. From the pictures he showed me, I do not doubt its effectiveness.

"CHUMMING" WITH OXYGEN

Building upon the success of his Oxygen Edge system (also discussed elsewhere), David Kinser has released a new product designed to "chum" fish with oxygen. It is called the "Oxy Chum" and it is worth discussing at length because it is such an off-the-wall concept.

"Believe it or not, fish can actually be chummed with dissolved oxygen," Kinser told me. "I'm talking chumming them up just like you would with fish parts or blood, except with pure oxygen."

This new unit is similar to his Oxygen Edge, which consists of a high-dollar filter, oxygen bottle, and diffuser, but it contains some intense technical modifications and a long hose to allow chumming in deep water to create what Kinser calls a "dissolved oxygen chum line."

The concept, while seemingly contrived, was actually born by accident while installing an oxygen system at a bait camp on the Bolivar Peninsula: "This guy had a big aerator running to a big tank full of mullet. All of the mullet were severely stressed with red noses, and they were on top of the water, gasping. After the oxygen system was on for a short while, the fish calmed down and were all gathered directly over the oxygen stone. They were in a 6-foot long tank, but every one of them was gathered around the bubbles. That's what first got me to thinking about creating an oxygen chumming system."

After considering this concept, several questions popped in my mind. The first was, in what type of setting does Kinser expected this

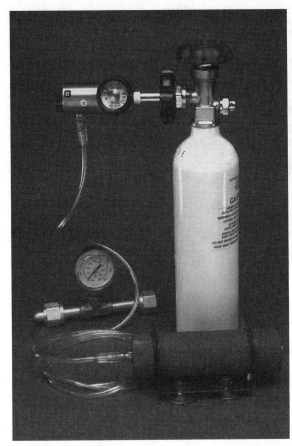

Oxygen Edge system

new system to work. Somehow, I just could not see drifting across the bay with an oxygen tube in the water attracting anything more than some odd stares from other anglers.

"This is going to be something that you have to use during the extremely hot months when there is little oxygen in the water, and around structure where fish are, like the offshore platforms or jetties," Kinser said. "You're going to use it just like you would when you throw out chum for fish and wait for them to follow the scent trail toward your position. The only difference is that they need oxygen more immediately than they need food. That is why when you are fishing offshore, the fish stay in a certain part of the water column during summer. That is where the oxygen is. Fish seek and stay where oxygen is. This will allow the angler to bring the oxygen to the fish."

The next question I asked was how much oxygen would it take to draw in fish. In a pond, it is easy to see how it might work, but in the open bay, the perspective broadens tremendously.

"The whole thing is that the envelope drifts with the current and

Oxy-chum in use.

fish can detect 1/10 of 1 part per million oxygen change," Kinser explained. "Offshore anglers in particular know what mashing up a few pogies can do. It creates an oil slick that spreads way out and draws in fish. The only difference is that oxygen is invisible, but it spreads much the same."

Kinser's confidence in his new product is not based strictly on personal observations and hypothesis. He has a couple of aces in the hole already: "Some of the top anglers on the Crappie USA tournament started using a prototype back in 1997 and did very well with it. Also, at a sports show, I met a commercial diver who uses oxygen bubbles to increase his buoyancy while underwater. He said he has major problems keeping fish like snapper and grouper away from him while diving. He told me they're drawn to the oxygen like a magnet."

This certainly is not a product that will gain widespread acceptance for flounder fishing, but it could gain a cult following if proven effective on a long-term basis.

SPEARFISHING

When flounder enter the waters of the Gulf of Mexico, spearfish-ermen occasionally kill them. I have talked with people who say that during winter months, the bottom of areas around oil platforms sitting in 100 feet of water is sometimes carpeted with flounder. One of the more interesting stories I have heard is about divers who spearfish giant halibut in Alaskan waters. They hit the fish with a spear equipped with an inflatable device that sends them up to the surface. Halibut are incredibly strong fish and wrestling with a 200-pounder on the bottom would be very dangerous.

The base of an oil rig can be a bountiful spot for spearfishing.

FOLLOWING DREDGES

Dredging operations churn up many things that flounder eat, like sand eels and marine worms. Some old timers say that fishing downcurrent of dredge operations can be very productive. I have never tried this one, but it could be worth checking out.

SMACKING THE WATER

While it is certain that flounder can hear, no one really knows how important a role hearing is in their feeding patterns. While researching this book, I came across an article describing a technique of fishing with live bait under a cork and slapping the water with a paddle. It did not say much other than that slapping the water with a paddle could attract flounder. Weird.

Chapter Four

The allure of lures

Plastic lures are common in flounder fishing circles. For years, many considered it a bit strange to seek flounder with anything but live bait, but over the last 10 years or so, anglers have switched to plastics in an almost revolutionary way.

I much prefer fishing soft plastics to live bait for flounder, and not because I prefer lure fishing. I like to use whatever gets the most fish to tug on my line, and in most cases, it is artificial lures.

Soft plastics are without a doubt the most reliable and consistently effective artificials for flounder. Their small size and ability to work on the bottom coupled with life-like action has great appeal to the predatory instincts of flounder. Since about 1995, I have done the majority of my flounder fishing with soft plastics, with the exceptions of testing new lures and for special situations like searching for trophy fish.

Soft plastics come in every shape, color, and size imaginable and are adaptable to just about any fishing situation. They allow you to "match the hatch," which means to imitate the size of prevalent bait-fishes during the different seasons. There are so many effective soft plastics out there that it is feasible to fish a small 3-inch shad imitation in the spring when flounder are preying on tiny menhaden, and go all the way up to an 8-inch double-tailed worm in autumn.

Hard lures are not good all-around flounder getters, but there are circumstances where they prove worthy. Sometimes, flounder feed aggressively on shallow flats and actually chase baitfishes. When they are up and feeding like this, they do not always go for soft plastic. It is during these times that shallow-running hard lures, spoons, or topwaters can be effective and add fun to your fishing.

LURE REVIEWS

The following are some artificial lures I have used for flounder, some for years. Some of them were suggested by experts, and others I tried as research for this book. There are simply too many lures to cover in one blanket statement, so I have provided a brief synopsis with each review. You can apply these to other similar lures.

The only general tip I will give involves soft plastics: Do not make big swings with your rod. Small 2- to 3-inch hops trigger the most bites. Otherwise, read the reviews and enjoy.

LURE: Old Bayside Speck Grub
COLOR: Glow with glowing chartreuse tail
BEST SEASON (S): Spring, summer, fall
APPLICATION/LOCATION: This lure is best fished on a 1/8- or 1/4-ounce jighead around the mouth of marsh points and along the shorelines of bay systems.

TECHNIQUE: Hop it slowly across the bottom or pitch it into cane stands and drag it slowly.

TIPS: This lure is most effective rigged perpendicular to the hook on the jighead, and tipped with a small piece of shrimp. I am a huge fan of tipping soft plastic lures with

Old Bayside Speck Grub

shrimp when flounder fishing, but while field-testing this lure, I caught flounder on it without tipping. The lure has a regular curl tail like my old favorite, the Twister Tail, which receives its due shortly, but there is a difference. This lure has a triple that imparts serious, serious action. Another plus is that the tail glows. Many baits with glow bodies and chartreuse tails do not have glowing tails. This chartreuse tail glows, and I believe that is a big plus.

LURE: Gambler Flappin' Shad

COLOR: Chartreuse

BEST SEASON (S): Summer, fall

APPLICATION/LOCATION: This is a good one to fish on the flats when flounder are actively feeding on large baitfishes.

TECHNIQUE: Rig this lure on a fish-finder (Carolina) rig and drag it slowly. Do not tip when Carolina rigging or it could ruin the action of the lure.

TIPS: Spray with a saltwater specific fish attractant.

Gambler Flappin' Shad

LURE: Twister Tail

COLOR: White, chartreuse, glow, pearl

BEST SEASON(S): Spring, summer, fall

APPLICATION/LOCATION: This lure is best fished on a 1/8- or 1/4-ounce jighead around the mouth of marsh points and along the shorelines of bay systems. This is not a good lure to fish in heavy-duty current.

TECHNIQUE: Drag slowly across the bottom or moderately hop it up and down.

TIPS: This lure is most effective rigged perpendicular to the hook on the jighead, and

Twister Tail

tipped with a small piece of shrimp. There is another version of this lure called the Spin Top combo that has a slightly different jighead and a small teardrop blade spinner fitted on it. It is hard to find, but an excellent choice.

LURE: Bass Pro Shops Offshore Angler Cajun Crab

BEST SEASON (S): Winter, early spring

COLOR: Glow, natural crab, bay crab

APPLICATION/LOCATION:

This lure works well as a "locator" bait during winter in deep holes in marshes and around outfall canals. Crab is a key component of floun- der diet in the winter and early spring, and I have friends who have had success on this lure.

TECHNIQUE: Fish it on a

Cajun Crab

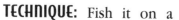

fish-finder (Carolina) rig or a free-line.

TIPS: Remember, small crabs float freely with the current quite a bit, so do not bog this one down with a heavy jighead. Let it look natural.

LURE: Berkley Inshore Power Tube

BEST SEASON(S): Year-round

COLOR: Pearl

APPLICATION/LOCATION: Work this one over sandy flats and along marsh edges.

TECHNIQUE: Rig it on a light jighead and drag slowly across the bottom.

TIPS: A neat trick is to stuff *Berkley Power Tube* the tube jig with pieces of Alka Seltzer and bits of shrimp. It will give off bubbles and can help attract fish.

LURE: Norton Sand Eel

BEST SEASON(S): Spring

COLOR: Glow/chartreuse, pearl

APPLICATION/LOCATION: This lure is a fine imitator of the sand eel, which is a chief prey item of flounder in early spring. It can catch flounder anywhere, but is best to fish over oyster reefs.

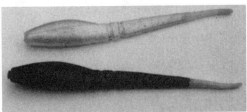

TECHNIQUE: The best way to rig this lure is to fish it on a 1/8-ounce jighead coupled with a Lindy No-Snagg Sinker for oyster reef fishing. These sinkers look weird, feel *Norton Sand Eel* weird, and, well, they are weird, but they work wonders for avoiding snags on oyster reefs.

TIPS: When fishing oyster reefs with this lure, try to keep your retrieve as slow as possible. Reefs are often located in areas with heavy current, and too fast of a retrieve can cause you to miss many fish. Also, do not expect to catch many flounder on an oyster reef. It is size that counts here. Keep in mind that structure holds flounder on reefs, so use your depthfinder to locate a huge clump of shell or perhaps a wreck. Mark that spot and work heavily with this lure.

LURE: B&L Corky

BEST SEASON(S): Spring, winter

COLOR: Chartreuse

APPLICATION/LOCATION: This lure is a slow-sinker, so fish it in areas that do not have lots of current. Flats and eddies in the mouths of marshy cuts are good places to fish this lure.

TECHNIQUE: Matagorda Bay guide Don Wood introduced this bait to me a few years ago. He said the only effective way to fish this lure is very, very slowly. Throw the lure out, let it sink, twitch it very gently, and let it hit the bottom. Flounder will hit this

Corky

lure on the fall most times. This lure is tremendous for catching flounder during winter when few anglers are actively seeking them. In fact, I would go so far as to say this is the best lure for winter flounder, especially those that follow baitfishes onto flats bordering the ship channel on warm days.

TIPS: Fish it slow, slow, slow.

LURE: Bill Lewis Slapstick

BEST SEASON(S): Spring, summer, fall

COLOR: Chrome, Chrome back, chartreuse shiner

APPLICATION/LOCATION: Fish this lure in shallow water where flounder are visibly feeding. Flats and shallow points are ideal.

TECHNIQUE: The lure sits upright in the water because of its shifted tail weight. Throw it near feeding flounder, pop once, and let sit. Repeat until successful.

TIPS: Allow flounder to take the lure underwater *Bill Lewis Slapstick*

before setting the hook, and when you do, set the hook very hard. Make sure and rig with braided or fusion line. Flounder hit lures on the surface differently and far more infrequently than they do on the bottom, so you will want to take all precautions to get a strong hookset.

LURE: Flounder Pounder

BEST SEASON(S): Spring, summer, fall

COLOR: White/pink, chartreuse, pink

APPLICATION/LOCATION: This lure is a multi-purpose flounder getter. The manufacturers designed it to be rigged with several different sinkers, so you can fish it in heavy current or areas with very little flow.

TECHNIQUE: I have had my best luck simply dragging this lure across the bottom, occasionally giving it a little pop.

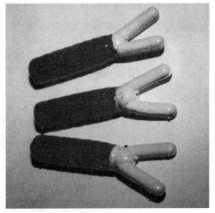

Flounder pounder

TIPS: It would not hurt to juice this lure up with some kind of fish attractant, like Fish Formula shrimp or shad flavor.

LURE: DOA Terror-Eyz

BEST SEASON(S): Spring, summer

COLOR: Chartreuse, white, red and white

APPLICATION/LOCATION: This is a good lure to pitch into stands of cane along shorelines and to work eddies.

TECHNIQUE: For best results, I usually slowly hop it across the bottom.

DOA Terror-Eyz

TIPS: The lure is designed for special jigheads with red protruding eyes. Therefore, I like to fish it in as clear water as possible to get the full effect.

LURE: Pygmy Spin

BEST SEASON(S): Spring

COLOR: Silver scale, fluorescent red/white

APPLICATION/LOCATION: This is a good spring lure to fish in areas with large concentrations of small menhaden, which flounder gorge themselves on this time of year.

TECHNIQUE: Fish with a slow retrieve by casting parallel to productive shorelines and into eddies.

TIPS: Do not be surprised to catch redfish on this lure. It is a killer for the ones that live in the marsh.

Pygmy Spin

LURE: Shad Assassin

BEST SEASON(S): Fall

COLOR: Chartreuse, pearl

Shad Assassin

APPLICATION/LOCATION: This one is good for areas on the main body of a bay system in front of marshy drains that are giving up lots of large menhaden, mullet, and shrimp. It is a big soft plastic, so it is best to fish it when baitfishes are at near-maximum size.

TECHNIQUE: Like many other soft plastics, this one is best fished on a jighead and bounced across the bottom.

TIPS: I caught one of my best flounder stringers ever on this lure by tipping it with shrimp.

LURE: Culprit DT Worm

BEST SEASON(S): Spring, summer, fall

COLOR: Pearl, tequila shad, pumpkinseed

APPLICATION/LOCATION:

This is a double-tailed worm designed for bass fishing, but it makes a great crossover into saltwater. I like to fish it in a current-laden area to give the lure more action.

Culprit DT Worm

TECHNIQUE: This is a go-to lure when the flounder simply will not bite anything else, but I know they are in the area. I use what is called a "dead worm" technique in bass fishing. It consists of throwing the lure out and letting it sit, then slowly retrieving and letting it sit again. In current, the tail gives up incredible action.

TIPS: Use a heavy jighead for heavy current. Go with at least 3/8-ounce up to 1/2-ounce as needed.

LURE: H&H Sparkle Beetles

BEST SEASON(S): Spring

COLOR: Chartreuse/glitter, white

APPLICATION/LOCATION: Fish this around cuts and along stands of

H&H Sparkle Beetles

roseau cane.

TECHNIQUE: Rig it on a 1/4-ounce jighead and hop slowly across the bottom.

LURE: Johnson 1/2-ounce spoon

BEST SEASON(S): Summer, fall

COLOR: Silver

APPLICATION/LOCATION: It is best to use this one on a flat where flounder are actively feeding. Do not use this lure to find flounder.

TECHNIQUE: Chunk it out,

Johnson 1/2-ounce spoon

reel it in by varying your retrieve. Throw to areas where flounder are visibly attacking baitfishes.

TIPS: It would not hurt to dress the lure with a red skirt or chartreuse Twister Tail trailer.

LURE: Berkley Power Mullet

BEST SEASON(S): Summer, fall

COLOR: Glow/chartreuse, purple/yellow for murky conditions

APPLICATION/LOCATION: This is a good lure for fishing in river systems above bays where flounder gather when salinity levels are high.

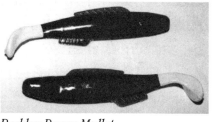
Berkley Power Mullet

TECHNIQUE: This is a good lure to use on a fish-finder (Carolina) rig or bounced on the bottom.

TIPS: Do not be afraid to let flounder take this lure. The manufacturer flavored it like a real fish, so it does not taste like plastic, and flounder will hold on longer.

LURE: Banjo Minnow
BEST SEASON(S): Summer, fall
COLOR: Natural minnow color
APPLICATION/LOCATION: This large lure is good to fish in heavy current. I would not hesitate to fish at jetties or in large drainages.

TECHNIQUE: Slowly drag lure across the bottom on a jighead or with a special Banjo Minnow weight.

TIPS: Possibly the liveliest lure I have seen. Do not overwork it because it moves enough on its own.

Banjo Minnow

LURE: Rip Tide weedless shrimp
BEST SEASON(S): Summer, early fall
COLOR: Smoke red mist, pearl glow, chartreuse
APPLICATION/LOCATION: Since it is weedless, this is a good lure in the marsh during the high tides of later summer and early fall. The marshes run thick with shrimp, and this is a good imitation in the marsh grass.

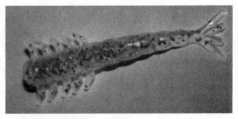

Rip Tide weedless shrimp

TECHNIQUE: Throw around clumps of grass in marsh and in areas with heavy vegetation. Aim for specific areas and work heavily.

TIPS: Do not be afraid to drag through heavy grass. The lure maker designed it for this kind of fishing.

LURE: CT Mullet

BEST SEASON(S): Spring, summer, fall

COLOR: Pumpkin/chartreuse/, glow/white

APPLICATION/LOCATION: This is a good lure to fish on oyster reefs in the spring and in heavy drains during summer and fall.

TECHNIQUE: Like most plastics, drag or bounce across the bottom.

TIPS: I like to rig this one per-pendicular to the hook.

CT Mullet

LURE: Sassy Shad

BEST SEASON(S): Spring, summer, fall

COLOR: Natural shad, pearl, chartreuse

APPLICATION/LOCATION: In spring, use the smallest version of the lure to fish in eddies where small baitfishes go to rest. During summer and fall, go to the big 5-inch to target flounder feeding on larger menhaden.

TECHNIQUE: Drag this lure slowly across bottom or hop it up and down.

Sassy Shad

TIPS: Be mindful of size for the different seasons. You have to match the hatch—small in spring, larger in summer and fall.

LURE: DOA Crab

BEST SEASON(S): Late fall/winter

COLOR: Brown, chartreuse

APPLICATION/LOCATION: Winter flounder fishing is usually very slow, but if you have to do it, this is a good lure choice. You are supposed to fish this lure extremely slowly, and that is what the metabolism is like of a flounder that stays in the bay this time of year.

TECHNIQUE: Drag very, very slowly across bottom.

TIPS: A flounder's diet will consist

DOA Crab

of many crustaceans this time of year, so do not feel weird for using it.

LURE: Catch-Em Lures' Sabine Snake

BEST SEASON (S): Spring

COLOR: Firetiger, junebug

APPLICATION/LOCATION: This lure imitates sand eels. You get best results on oyster reefs in spring.

TECHNIQUE: Fish it on a breakaway rig or bounce it on a hefty jighead.

TIPS: Do not expect to catch many flounder on oyster reefs. Just expect to catch big ones.

Catch-Em Lures' Sabine Snake

LURE: Pradco Spit-N-Image

BEST SEASON (S): Fall

COLOR: Tennessee shad, red/white

APPLICATION/LOCATION: This is an effective lure only when flounder are actively feeding.

TECHNIQUE: Throw out lure, pop it a few times, and reel in a few feet. Repeat process until successful.

TIPS: You do not need to "walk the dog" for topwater flounder.

Pradco Spit-N-Image

SETTING THE HOOK

Hookset with artificial lures is much different from with the real thing. Whereas with a live mud minnow, you might want to wait 10 seconds to set the hook, with a Twister Tail, you need to wait just a second or two. Flounder simply hit lures differently and will spit them out if you do not get a quick hookset.

Hookset is an overlooked dynamic in flounder fishing. These fish have extremely bony mouths and are just plain hard to put a hook into, which is why I recommend braided or fusion line for lure fishing. When you go to set the hook into a flounder, do so with great force. Do not be afraid to make a hard, sweeping hookset. These are not speckled trout with paper mouths. They are flounder and have a completely different kind of mouth structure. This goes for the hard lures, too. When a flounder attacks a spoon or topwater, do not be afraid to set the hook on impact.

ENHANCING LURES

When fishing many soft plastic lures, I like to tip the jig with shrimp. This gives the flounder a reason to hold onto a plastic lure, plus it leaves a scent trail to entice a flounder to get up and follow the lure. Be sure to get shrimp that are in good condition. If they look like they have been left in the sun for a long time, do not waste your time. Remember that 90 percent of the scent in a shrimp is located in the tail section. Use scissors to cut a piece of the tail into small pieces. Cover the exposed hook to enhance the chances of a good hookup.

Some flounder have very little belly meat, which makes that part of the body poor for filleting but great for enhancing your lures. Cut the belly meat off in strips and leave the skin on. Use this to tip jigs. It is very popular on the East Coast and worked well the times I tried it.

Chapter
Five

Live bait & tactics

Live bait is the traditional method for catching flounder. Over the years, I have tried many different live types of bait. Some are effective for just about any fishing scenario, while others are very situation-specific. Many anglers feel that flounder lie on the bottom waiting to hit anything that you put in front of them. Any flounder could possibly hit any bait at any given time, so that is true in a roundabout way. However, to use live bait successfully, you have to use the right bait at the right time.

GULF KILLIFISH (MUD MINNOW, COCAHOE)

Mud minnows are without a doubt the most popular and probably the all-around best flounder bait. These small marsh dwellers are abundant in flounder territory year-round, and a regular part of the natural diet. Mud minnows are a very hardy fish that can be hooked several ways: through both lips, behind the dorsal fin, or through the body near the tail.

Most anglers fish mud minnows on a fish-finder (Carolina) rig and drag them slowly across the bottom. The general rule is to wait 10 seconds after the flounder first hits to set the hook.

Possibly the biggest advantage to using mud minnows is that they are available year-round at most coastal bait shops.

MULLET

Mullet, especially the small ones known as finger mullet, are just as good for flounder fishing, although they are difficult to find at bait

shops. You usually have to catch your own with a casting net. You can hook mullet the same way as mud minnows, but they usually do not live as long. It is best to use mullet in summer and fall when they are most abundant in the coastal ecosystem.

If you want to catch mullet in one particular area on a

regular basis, try baiting with canned dog food or bread. Mullet will gather around these spots and are easy to find. Most of the ones you see on the surface are the big ones, but there should be plenty of finger mullet there as well.

GULF MENHADEN

Menhaden, also known as pogey or shad, are another good flounder bait. The drawback is they are very difficult to keep alive in a livewell or on the hook; live ones are virtually impossible to find at a bait camp. A cast net is a necessity in retrieving this small baitfish. During spring, menhaden is very effective for catching flounder because that is their chief prey item during that time of year.

Something to keep in mind about menhaden is they do not necessarily have to be alive to be effective. If they are fresh and dead, they will still catch flounder. To keep dead ones fresh, put them on top of several layers of ice and do not let them get overly wet.

CROAKER

Very few anglers use small croaker for flounder bait, but they are an excellent choice and maybe as effective as mullet and minnows. I learned this by accident a couple of years ago. I have a 500-gallon aquar-

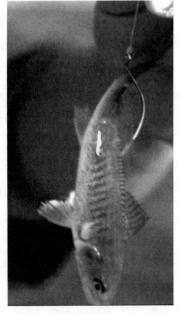

ium that my father built for me for fish observation. At the time, I was keeping six flounder in it. I went speckled trout fishing and had about three-dozen small 4- to 6-inch croaker left in my livewell. I scooped them up and put them in the aquarium so they would stay alive for the next trip. They did not make it.

As soon as the first croaker made it to the bottom of the tank, the flounder went wild. The biggest specimen gulped the croaker up and an all-out feeding frenzy began. Within a few minutes, there were only about a dozen left; by the next morning, only one.

Since then, I have used small croaker for flounder on several occasions and always caught fish. Croaker are easy to find at bait shops, and they usually have a long hook life. They often show up in the stomachs of flounder. Croaker is good bait year-round.

LIVE SHRIMP

Live shrimp is great flounder bait. They stay lively in livewells and active on a hook, and they are a top prey item for flounder most of the year. The only drawback to shrimp is that virtually everything in the bay eats them, making them difficult to keep on the hook for long in flounder territory.

MARINE WORMS

Occasionally a bait camp will carry marine worms. These creatures are a top prey item for flounder during the spring run, when the nasty-looking creatures are most abundant. A.C. Becker addressed using night crawlers in place of marine worms in his book, *Flounder: How, When & Where*, and made a good point. Yes, they can be effective, but they do not live well in saltwater and small baitfishes gobble them up quickly.

I experimented with using marine worms in March 2002 and caught three flounder on them. That was three flounder in an entire morning of fishing, while my partner caught four times that many. In short, it works but not enough to put a lot of fish in the livewell. Stick with the other baits here unless you are simply in the mood for something strange.

FIDDLER CRAB

Flounder eat lots of crab, particularly during winter and early spring when other baitfishes are not available. Fiddler crabs in particular are good flounder baits and easy to gather around boat docks and along marshy roads. Flounder gladly accept a hooked fiddler, but a sheepshead or redfish might get to it first; they are crab-eating specialists.

LIVELY BAIT IS BEST

The trick to using live bait is to keep it alive. A dead baitfish is not nearly as enticing as something that wiggles around. For land-bound anglers, a large Styrofoam ice chest will do a good job keeping most baitfishes kicking. Styrofoam breathes, and if the water is changed periodically, most bait will do well. For anglers in boats, a recirculating livewell is the ideal setup. By exchanging water frequently, anglers can achieve low bait mortality most of the time.

Adding stabilizing chemicals to the water can extend bait life significantly. Sure-Life Laboratories makes Pogey-saver, Croaker-Saver, Shrimp-Saver, and other chemical additives specifically for mullet and many other baitfishes. A cou-

Pogey-Saver

ple of spoonfuls of this stuff eliminates ammonia from the water, which is produced by the baitfishes themselves and, if left unchecked, will kill them.

Oxygen is the key component in keeping anything alive, particularly baitfishes. In more than 30 years of research, Texas Parks and Wildlife Department (TPWD) biologists have found that low levels of dissolved oxygen kills more fish in Texas waters than any other single cause. Biologists suspect low amounts of dissolved oxygen causes 60 percent of all fish and wildlife mortality in Texas waters. These hypoxia (oxygen deprivation) related moralities seem to be far more prevalent in saltwater. Some 56 percent of the habitat affected by a lack of oxygen is in the Gulf of Mexico, 30 percent is in estuaries, and only 14 percent is in freshwater lakes and streams.

The potential for fish morality increases dramatically during the summer months when rising water temperatures contribute to lower oxygen levels in coastal waters. David Kinser of Anahuac, Texas, has a unique insight into these phenomena that all anglers can benefit from.

Kinser, who is an avid angler, has spent more than two decades creating and modifying human life support systems for the medical field and has developed an uncanny understanding of the links between oxygen, life and death: "Oxygen is quite simply the key to all life. Without it, nothing can live. That is why all of these space probes and satellites we are sending out into the galaxy are looking for signs of oxygen on other planets. Without oxygen, life as we know it cannot exist."

Kinser, who owns Oxygenation Systems of Texas, has garnered quite a reputation among live bait enthusiasts and bass tournament anglers for his "Oxygen Edge" fish and bait oxygenation system. Instead of relying on standard aeration to keep bait or tournament fish alive, Kinser's system involves super-charging the water with pure oxygen: "Standard aeration systems draw from the air, which is composed of 21 percent oxygen. Factor in that many units only achieve 65 to 80 percent efficiency, and it becomes obvious what happens when water temperatures start to heat up. The fish start to die because they are not getting enough oxygen."

I have had an Oxygen Edge unit since early 1998, and I can attest to their absolute effectiveness. Speaking very conservatively, I can say that I have been able to reduce live bait mortality by 80 percent using the Edge.

Another advantage of using the Edge is that it keeps baitfish "supercharged." The oxygen keeps their metabolism so high that they are very frisky and more likely to attract a response for a flounder or other predatory fishes.

DISSECTING THE FLOUNDER BITE

Flounder do not bite like a redfish or trout, which usually hit a bait and start running with it. Flounder usually "thump" bait and then hold it in their bony mouth before swallowing. Through captive observation, I have watched them attack live bait, back off, and attack it again. This is why most live-baiters have adopted the 10-second rule: Get the thump, count to 10. and set the hook.

Flounder are unique in that they will bite for two reasons: hunger and intrusion of territory. A hungry flounder will get up after bait and might actively seek it, following after it picks up a scent trail. This is when they are actively feeding. An intrusion of territory bite is a very different concept. Since flounder are territorial and lie on the bottom most of the time, they can be angered into biting. When flounder stop biting, work over key areas very intensely. Throw to proven locations repeatedly and you could find fish. By putting the bait right on top of flounder, you are almost forcing them to bite. Usually, an angry bite is more aggressive and does not require the 10-second rule.

RIGGING UP

Many anglers use hooks too big for most practical purposes. By using a small hook, you avoid impaling the vital organs of a baitfish and impeding its action in the water. Bait will usually live longer when fished on a small hook. No. 4 or 6 treble hooks or 3/0 Kahle-style single hooks are good for most live baits.

Leaders are another important consideration. Flounder have sharp teeth, which can cut through thin monofilament very easily. However, their teeth are not as sharp as a shark's nor the bite as powerful, so does not require steel wire. I use 20- to 25-pound-test monofilament as a shock leader and have very few cut-offs.

Sinkers come in many shapes, sizes, and weights, and prescribing them blindly is a bit challenging. A good rule of thumb is to use pyramid sinkers for deep areas with heavy current, and egg sinkers for flats and most other areas.

Most of the time, flounder fishing is on the bottom, which makes sense because that is where flounder live. However, sometimes the bottom has too many snags, so floating rigs are used. There is not any magic way to rig a floating flounder rig. The best way I have found is to use a saltwater popping cork rigged above a Kahle-style hook with a split shot weight about 6 inches above it. Make sure the bait is getting down to no more than 6 inches above the bottom, else the flounder probably will not go after it. This rig is great for fishing with menhaden or around bulkheads and heavy reefs.

I have found that flounder in fast-moving deep water are not line shy, whereas those in shallow, clear water are. Keep that in mind when rigging up.

Chapter Six

Gigging: A flatfish tradition

Bill Phelps of Corpus Christi is rarely home on calm nights during the summer and fall. He is usually prowling the clear waters of Laguna Madre with a lantern in one hand and a flounder gig in the other.

"I am addicted to flounder gigging. It is a sport I started as a teenager and I have not been able to stop. I'd rather gig than fish any day of the week," Phelps said.

A strong cult following shares that sentiment and considers the pursuit more thrilling and fulfilling than anything else on the coast. Diehard rod and reel anglers might not understand, but gigging is something that gets in your blood.

"A bad night out gigging beats a good day of chunking bait or lures any day of the week," Phelps said.

The allure of gigging probably has a lot to do with the very nature of the sport. It is a lot more like hunting than fishing, and in writ-

51

ing about flounder fishing over the years, I have found many giggers are also avid hunters. Giggers have to stalk and approach flounder with stealth. Flounder are very vulnerable to this technique because they feed at night in shallow, clear water where giggers can spot them.

The process may sound simple, but there are many details to this game that make it challenging and sometimes even a bit dangerous. Flounder gigging can get quite sophisticated. Serious giggers (especially commercial ones) mount lights on the front of a flat-bottomed boat and use a push pole to quietly navigate shallow water. I have seen boats with huge floodlights that go out to the sides and lights hanging from all directions.

All of that gear is really cool and effective, but it is not necessary. In fact, many veteran giggers prefer simpler gear: a johnboat, gig, and waterproof light. Any johnboat will work, as will any powerful light.

Gig style is a matter of preference, and I like a two-pronged head. Some people like a single prong, but I can hold down bigger fish with a double. Some giggers use three- and four-pronged gigs. Again, it is all personal preference; they all get the job done in the end.

On incoming tides, flounder feed in shallows and on sandy flats. Look for them on calm, dark nights around mouths of cuts and along marshy shorelines. Hunting them on a calm night is very important because ripples on the water greatly reduce visibility.

Looking for flounder on the bottom can be challenging. Giggers look for anything unusual, like an outline or eyes reflecting in the light. It is very important to make sure you are looking at a flounder before gigging it. Stingrays conceal themselves in the same way and in the same places at night, and they can deliver a very nasty blow with their "stinger." One sure-fire way to tell if the creature is a stingray is to look for a thin whip-like tail attached to it. In addition, if the creature is 3 feet wide, it is not a flounder.

It is best to use your strong hand to hold the gig. When you find a flounder, give it a good strong stab so that the points of the prongs stick into the ground. Flounder or ray, it will flap about madly. It is very important to keep pressure on the fish until it settles down. Once the water clears, locate the head and prepare to bring the fish up. I say "locate the head" because flounder have nasty teeth and you do not want to get bitten. It has happened to me before while attempting to remove a hook; it hurt, bad. To pick up the fish, slide your hand underneath and feel for the metal prongs, then lift.

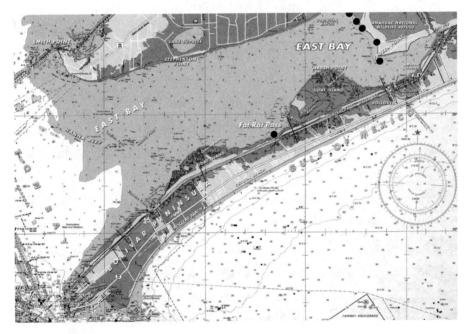

East Galveston gigging hotspots

Flounder are abundant in all Texas bay systems, but some spots produce better for giggers, especially during the fall migration. Corpus Christi Bay and surrounding waters harbor good numbers of flatfish. Giggers prowl the clear waters along the shoreline of the main bay on calm nights, and regularly stringer limits of big flounder. On the main body of the bay, rock jetties line the shoreline. These spots are accessible from the bank and can be highly productive at certain times.

Flounder expert Capt. Don Hand ranks Laguna Madre as one of the real sleeper spots for flounder. He told me some of the best spots are around the Land Cut and in the Intracoastal Canal where shallow shorelines meet a steep drop-off.

Sabine Lake is probably the all-around best flounder destination on the Gulf Coast, but the gigging runs hot and cold because of water clarity. I advise giggers to target the eastern shoreline, which has more than 20 cuts that empty more than 100,000 acres of marsh.

Other key areas include East Pass, the Intracoastal Canal from Burton's Ditch south to Stewt's Island, Sydney Island, and the outfall side of the Entergy Canal.

The East Galveston/Trinity Bay complex offers an overwhelming array of flounder habitat by virtue of its sheer size. One of the hottest spots is Rollover Bay just behind Rollover Pass, and the Intracoastal Canal in the same area.

The Anahuac Refuge shoreline is another sure bet for flounder. Secondary spots for gigging are Smith's Point, Chocolate Bayou, and the south shoreline of East Galveston Bay. Like Sabine Lake, the gigging runs hot and cold due to water clarity.

The Texas City flats on Galveston Bay proper are another fruitful flounder gigging location from time to time, as are the shorelines in the Kemah/Seabrook area.

Some of the most fascinating stories I have heard regarding flounder come from giggers of the past. One of the best came from Bill Vasek of Vidor, who used to gig extensively in the 50 and 60s. He told me that while gigging around Louisiana's Lake Calcasieu, he and 11 other men collected 800 flounder in one night. They were going gigging to get meat for a fish fry, and ended up getting more than they bar-

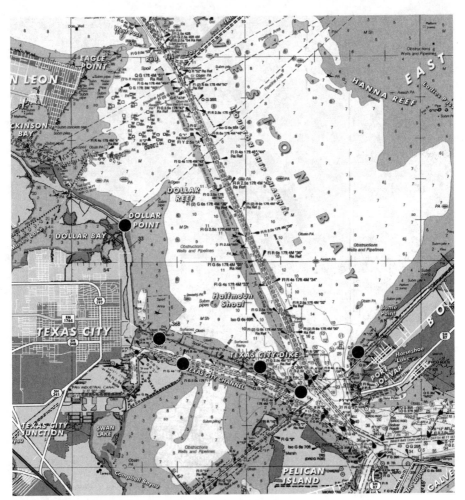

Texas City gigging hotspots

gained for. Thank goodness we have limits in place nowadays, but you have to admit there is a certain romance to such stories.

The late Dan Rebsamen told me of gigging a flounder "nearly three feet long" in South Bay back in the 1950s. He said it took him and his friend both wrestling with it to get it in the boat. They, of course, ate the fish and never had it weighed on official scales. I would almost join a monastery to get a crack at such a flounder. (Well, not really, but you know what I mean.)

PHOTO COURTESY OF CAPT. MARK TALASEK

Chet Talasek gigs a big Matagorda Bay flounder on a specially-rigged gigging boat operated by his father, Capt. Mark Talasek.

If you are tired of standard rod and reel fishing tactics, consider flounder gigging. It is a very different experience, and one of the most effective ways of bringing flounder fillets to the table. That alone has immense value.

Chapter Seven

Tides mean everything to flounder

Tides are important to the feeding and movement of all saltwater life forms, from blue crabs to bull sharks. However, no game species ties more closely to the tides than flounder. Tides dictate every facet of their lives somehow, and the moment anglers realize this, they become more successful at finding and catching flounder—I guarantee that.

As noted elsewhere in this book, flounder are lazy fish that lie on the bottom and ambush prey that swims or drifts near. In other words, they wait for the tide to bring food to them instead of going out looking for it. Flounder are not good swimmers and rarely do it more than necessary.

Before we get into how to best use the tide tables to aid your flounder fishing, let's look at exactly how tides work.

One of the questions I hear most often from readers, goes something like: "I saw where the low tide was going to be an 11:15, but the water was up above the boat dock. How could the tide be so high during the low tide period?"

To answer this and most other questions about tides, consider what tides are and exactly what forces cause them. Tides are the periodic rise and fall of all ocean waters. Nature causes them in two different ways: gravity from the moon and sun, and gravity from Earth.

My mentor, veteran outdoor writer Ed Holder, told me that the easiest way to understand how these tidal movements work is to compare them to a wave: "In essence, a tide is a large, slow-moving wave that starts off in the ocean, moves through a pass, and ends up in the back of a bay or upland into a river system. And it is all influenced by the elements."

Remember that wind influences most waves and tides are no different. This is why some low tides are not always low. A strong southerly wind pushes a lot of water into a bay system, causing unusually high tides, sometimes even during periods when moon or solar patterns dictate a low tide. When strong south winds are prevalent, it plays havoc with tide tables. What is supposed to be low tide can be more than a foot above normal because of constant, pounding south wind. Conversely, north winds push water out of the bays. This is why we get such low tides during the fall. "Blue northers" in conjunction with a strong tidal pull really drains an area and helps cleanse coastal marshes.

Moving on but keeping with the idea of the tide as a wave, it is very important to understand that tidal strength at points away from the immediate coastline will not be as strong as those at a pass near the Gulf.

"You've got to realize that like any wave, a tide weakens as it moves inland," Holder told me. "Your strongest tide will be near the Gulf, and the weakest will be far into the bay or river."

In the *Port Arthur News*, we give tides for the Old Coast Guard station at Sabine Pass. At Stewt's Island, on the north end of Sabine Lake, a 3-foot tidal change at the pass may be reduced to somewhere between 2 and 2-1/2 feet. In addition, 10 miles upriver at the Interstate 10 Bridge on the Neches River, it might be only a 1-foot change. Remember, the wave weakens as it moves farther inland.

Another question I am frequently asked is: "We saw on the television where we would have a high tide about 5:00 a.m., so we got out there an hour early and the tide didn't move for hours. Was the TV tide table wrong?"

Probably not. Most times when I get a question like this, it is from someone who does not understand one very important point about tides: tides as reported in some newspapers and on television merely tell you when the lows and highs occur. They do not tell you how much change will occur between tides. Say for a Tuesday, the tables predict two high tides and two low tides. The highs will occur at 3:35 a.m. and 12:58 p.m., and the lows at 8:55 a.m. and 8:37 p.m. That is all the information you get in some tide tables. However, if you dig deeper into charts that the National Weather Service maintains, you find some very interesting information about those same tides. You learn that the tide will drop only 8 inches between the 3:35 am. high and 8:55 a.m. low, and the forecast calls for it to rise only about 5 inches between the 8:55 a.m. low and 12:50 p.m. high. You also learn that between the 12:50 p.m. high and 8:37 p.m. low, the tide should drop more than 2-1/2 feet, which is a very strong tide for the Texas Gulf Coast.

Now, let's suppose someone decides to go fishing on that Tuesday morning and does not look at our tidal chart, but instead glances at the tide times on television. He sees there will be a low tide at 8:55 a.m. and a high tide at 12:50 p.m., so he assumes the tide at the Port Isabel jetties will be rising between those two times. It will, but it will rise only 5 inches, which is an inch an hour. He probably will not even notice the change, and will come back convinced the television was wrong.

To base a fishing trip around tidal movements, the key thing to watch is how much change will occur between tides. Just reading the general tide table is a waste of time. An angler must use the tidal correction table to adjust for tidal movements in the area he plans to fish. Once you learn how to read tide charts, there are some things to keep in mind that can help you fish around tides. It is important to watch the charts for quick tidal turnarounds and swings from one extreme to the other in a short period. The faster the water is moving, the more prey is displaced from its cover and put into the open water.

Jetty fishing is often more productive along the Gulf side during an incoming tide, but the action usually shifts to channel side on an outgoing. This is because shrimp, shad, and other baitfishes exit the bay toward the Gulf.

Remember that tidal movement is always most out of proportion and visible around passes and inlets. That is because water in these narrow areas passes through powerfully. In the bays or in the ocean it is not always easy to tell when the current is moving or in which direction. Sometimes there is a conflict between wind and tide, and on a weak tide with a strong wind, it can be especially hard to tell which force is moving which way. A good way to find which way the tide is moving is to find some structure and look for signs of movement around it. If you are wading, you can kick up some sand and see which direction it settles. If you are in a boat, you can pitch out a lightweight sinking lure and see which way it moves.

Now that you have accurate information, about let's take a basic look at how tides affect flounder.

As noted earlier in the chapter, tidal movements affect flounder more than any other species. That is because they cannot corral and assault prey species in open water like speckled trout do. Their existence revolves around intercepting baitfishes that cruise over a given point. When tides move menhaden, shrimp, croaker, mullet, and other prey species through an area, flounder are stimulated to feed. Big, incoming tides provide the best flounder fishing during spring and summer, and outgoing tides provide the best action in the fall when cold fronts blow large amounts of water and baitfishes out of marshes and into bay systems.

Let us start with the incoming tides.

Most anglers will tell you that outgoing tides are best for flounder fishing; during fall, they are. Nevertheless, from February through September, I much prefer fishing an incoming tide because it concentrates flounder at the mouths of cuts leading into the marsh, and when they are at these spots, they are easiest to catch. The first thing I look for on an incoming tide is an "eddy" or area of slack water at the mouth of the cut. These are by far the best spots to catch flounder on an incoming tide because baitfishes that cannot negotiate the fast water end up there, and flounder lie in ambush. If there is one running theme to this book, it is that flounder are lazy and opportunistic and will go where they have to work the least in order to eat. Eddies are such places, especially on incoming tides.

A prime example is on Louisiana's Lake Calcasieu on the Cameron Prairie shoreline, where anglers catch massive numbers of redfish around the weir structures. I fished these weirs for reds in the summer of 2003, and after making a few casts at the schooling redfish, I noticed a big eddy on the edge of the weir and many menhaden in the water. I grabbed a rod baited with a soft plastic shad imitation and chunked into the eddy. After slowly dragging it across the bottom for a few seconds, I felt the famous flounder "thump" and began what ended up a magnificent flounder catch. There were two of us in the boat, and we came home with 12 flounder ranging from 14 to 21 inches. On that particular day, there were very few small ones and we were truly happy anglers. Later that week, I wrote an article for the *Port Arthur News* about that trip, how the incoming tide turned on the flounder bite, and how we fished the eddies. I later received an email from a reader confused by what I wrote. He was sure I had mistakenly written "incoming" instead of "outgoing." When I responded that I prefer incoming tides, he was shocked and admitted he had missed a lot of good fishing over the years. I still get email from him and he never misses a chance to fish the incoming tides.

Outgoing tides can also be very fruitful for flounder fishing. During the fall, they are obviously good because cold fronts purge the marshes, sending shrimp and baitfishes through the cuts where floun-

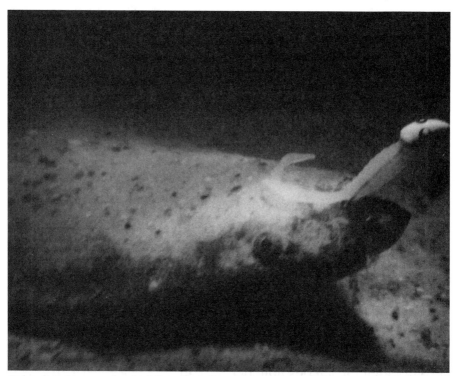

Tides dictate every facet of flounder's lives somehow, and the moment anglers realize this, they become more successful at finding and catching flounder.

der can easily attack them. They can also be good during spring and summer, but you have to rethink you strategy. Sure, you can catch flounder in the mouths of cuts on outgoing tides, sometimes lots of them, but I have a lot more luck fishing the shorelines.

Outgoing tides first bring baitfishes out of the marshes and eventually into the main bay. When the tides start getting to where they cover the edge of the cane stands on the shorelines, baitfishes start hiding there. I am a huge fan of targeting roseau cane stands, where I flip a jig tipped with shrimp and work it back to the boat. Flounder are waiting for the tides to fall and baitfishes to come out. In the first hour or two of an outgoing tide, I get far better action on the shorelines fishing in front of roseau cane stands than I do in the mouths of cuts.

In fall when marshes purge, the most obvious spots to fish during an outgoing tide are the mouths of cuts, but do not limit yourself to fishing these locations. A few years ago, while filming an episode of Keith Warren's popular *Texas Angler* TV program, we got ran off Sabine Lake by brutal winds. We ended up in the old Sabine River channel, and as we looked for a spot to fish, I noticed a small island that stood out in front of the marsh. Where the moving water rushed out of one particular point of the island, I could see something terrorizing the baitfishes. We stopped there and ended up with a Texas limit of flounder within an hour. Ever since, I have paid attention to such locations in the fall and always had success doing so. Any small island or peninsula gives flounder a spot to ambush baitfishes, which often follow whatever structure along the shoreline out toward open water. If you look around, there are hundreds of these spots on bay systems and the rivers leading to them, and many of them are likely to produce serious flounder results.

In general, the biggest tides provide the best fishing, no matter if they are high or low; the bigger the better. In fact, as far as I am concerned, you cannot beat a huge tide caused by a tropical storm. Storm tides provide some of the most outstanding flounder fishing of the year. When water levels begin to rise in marshy cuts, flounder that inhabit the main body of a bay and those that bond to the shoreline will stack up in the mouths of the cuts to take advantage of the great influx of bait-fishes entering the shallower, protected waters.

During a mild tropical storm that hit the Upper Texas Coast in September 1998, Sabine Lake Capt. Skip James (whom you will get to know fairly well in this book) and I took out Mr. Twister sales representative Darryl Laurent and his son to fish on the Louisiana side of Sabine Lake. Parts of Freeport were hit pretty hard, but all we got was heavy rain and big tides, so James and I were foaming at the mouth to go after flounder. We knew there would be a strong bite. Our first stop was at the mouth of Bridge Bayou, where we immediately noticed a large whirlpool forming in the current on the lee side of the cut. As the rain beat down in sheets, we cast our jigs into this whirlpool and picked up five flounder in as many casts. With our general strategy of "stick and move," we moved up a few yards into the cut and caught flounder after flounder. Within two hours, we had caught more than 40 flounder. We kept 10 of the biggest to bring home and eat and released the others to fight another day. We were the only boat out on the water that day. The crab trappers were not even out. When we pulled into the marina looking like a group of drowned rats, an old man asked if we were crazy. "Like a fox," I said, knowing that our knowledge of tides allowed us to have one of the most incredible days of fishing any of us had ever experienced.

If you heed but one piece of advice from this book, let it be this: Learn the tides in your area and use them to your advantage. They are what cause flounder to bite and be in particular locations, and consequently land flounder in your cooler—and I know that is where you want them to be.

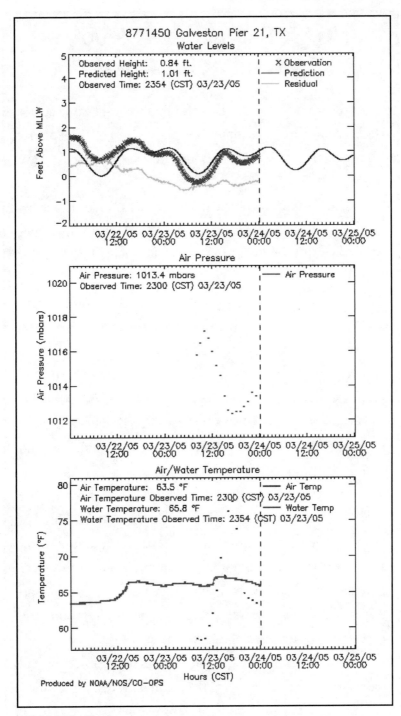

NOAA Tide Chart

65

NOAA EXPLAINS THE MOON'S EFFECTS ON TIDES

In researching the moon's effects on tides, I came across this from the National Oceanic and Atmospheric Administration (NOAA). It is the best explanation I have found:

At the surface of the earth, the earth's force of gravitational attraction acts in a direction inward toward its center of mass, and thus holds the ocean water confined to this surface.

However, the gravitational forces of the moon and sun also act externally upon the earth's ocean waters. These external forces are exerted as tide-producing, or so-called "tractive" forces. Their effects are superimposed upon the earth's gravitational force and act to draw the ocean waters to positions on the earth's surface directly beneath these respective celestial bodies (i.e., towards the "sublunar" and "subsolar" points).

High tides are produced in the ocean waters by the "heaping" action resulting from the horizontal flow of water toward two regions of the earth representing positions of maximum attraction of combined lunar and solar gravitational forces. Low tides are created by a compensating maximum withdrawal of water from regions around the earth midway between these two humps.

The alternation of high and low tides is caused by the daily (or diurnal) rotation of the earth with respect to these two tidal humps and two tidal depressions.

Chapter Eight

Seasonal patterns

SPRING RUN

Mention spring flounder run to many anglers, and you are likely to a blank stare or a puzzled look. For many years, most articles written about flounder fishing centered almost entirely on the fall run, when flounder exit the bays for the Gulf of Mexico to spawn. Until I started penning articles on flounder back in the early 1990s, there was very little mention of anything in spring.

If you think about it, a spring run makes perfect sense. If they leave *en masse* annually, it is logical they will eventually return. They return as winter loosens its grip and water temperatures climb in the coastal ecosystem, and the daily photoperiod changes. This is when flounder begin to migrate into bay systems from Gulf spawning grounds.

The spring run is different from the fall migration in that the flounder move back into the bays in short, but steady bursts. Tens of thousands of flounder might move out of a bay in fall during the course of one day, but only a couple of thousand might enter it during a given spring day. The spring run may actually begin as early as February in some areas and continue into May.

I have broken the spring run down into three sections to make it clear what is going on and when are your best chances for catching large numbers of trophy sized flatfish.

EARLY RUN

Over years of study and hardcore fishing, I have found that flounder actually start to enter bay systems between the first and second week of February. Mark your calendar on the days of the highest tide and when the full moon falls during this period. This is the catalyst for the migration and it can get you catching limits of flounder before your friends are even aware they are in the bays.

I first noticed this phenomenon in the late '90s and verified this during a careful angling study I conducted in February of the years 2000-2003. The first encounter with limits of flounder in February occurred while seeking redfish for a photo shoot at Burton's Ditch on the Sabine River. Upon flipping a chartreuse-colored, curl-tailed grub along some grass on the outer edge of this cut, I received a massive "thump." Shortly, I netted a 3-pound flounder, one of more than 20 flatfish I would catch that day. Only a few of these flounder were under-sized, and the largest weighed close to 5 pounds.

What were these flounder doing way up the Sabine River during the second week of February? (I fished this spot mostly during late spring and into summer.) Secondly, why were all of these fish so big? It is a rare occurrence to catch so many big flounder during one trip anymore.

I decided to fish spots in the Sabine River, along the Louisiana shoreline of Sabine Lake, and over on Lake Calcasieu three times a week during the first and second week of February. I also called all of the bait camps from Calcasieu to Rockport to see if I could find any kind of pattern. The results were astounding. I found that during those four consecutive Februaries, I caught the biggest flounder of each of those years and in good numbers. Main cuts in the bay and areas along the ship channel produced fish, but the Sabine River was the best—simply red hot on several trips.

Beginning with the second week of February, flounder reports increased all along the coast. The problem was there were very few anglers fishing during this time, but upon questioning bait camp owners, it was easy to see the flounder action spiked. I continued gathering reports on into April and found out that numbers decreased around Easter, and the average size decreased as well.

Upon talking with my mentor, veteran outdoor writer Ed Holder, I learned he had experienced similar patterns over the years and had came to the same conclusion I had. The biggest flounder migrate first, feed heavily to restore fat reserves lost during the migration, and then disperse within an ecosystem.

A final word on early migration is not to greatly fear late winter/early spring flooding situations. Flounder can tolerate freshwater very well, and I believe super fresh conditions do not make much of a difference in the early migration into the upper reaches of bays and river mouths, as I have caught them in good numbers during flood times.

Before we move onto the next phase of spring fishing, it is worth noting that some bait camps will not carry mud minnows during late winter, so your live bait options are limited. I prefer lure fishing anyway, and mostly use a glow or chartreuse-colored 4-inch Twister Tail tipped with shrimp. These are the only colors I use when I am not test-ing lures, but there is an exception. When the water is just nasty look-ing, I use a junebug-colored plastic. I have found this color will get strikes in super muddy water when nothing else will. I prefer not fish-ing in these conditions, but sometimes, if you want to catch fish, you have no choice. It's either deal with the situation at hand or go home. I vote for adapting and overcoming.

THE REAL SPRING RUN

The early run is fascinating, but most of the peak action is during March and April. Locating spring flounder is easy. Concentrate your first efforts in the mouths of cuts leading into bays from large marsh systems. Look for cuts that are wide enough and deep enough to flush lots of marsh water on tidal movements. Try the first couple of major points, eddies, and the first "S" turn inside tributaries with moving water. Flounder typically haunt the edge line of such areas.

Baitfishes, like juvenile menhaden, which are not yet strong

Flounder look for deep, wide cuts.

enough this time of year to fight the currents, rest in the slack water. It is very important to not overlook this predator/prey relationship during spring. Many anglers mistakenly look for larger baitfishes like mullet and big menhaden to find flounder, but that is not the way to go in spring. During this time of year, flounder are after menhaden. Flounder are opportunists and go after the easiest thing to catch and during spring, which is menhaden.

As I noted in another chapter, tides dictate how flounder feed. On a fast falling tide, they move in close to the drainage in tight schools. When it is falling slowly, they might scatter out around the mouth of a specific drainage or up into the marsh. They do the same thing during the first hour or so of an incoming tide. Then they usually move into the cuts.

Another good area to look for spring flounder is along the main shorelines of bay systems. Attacking vast shorelines would be a waste of time and end up in dogged frustration, so you have to have a strategy. Instead of looking over eight miles of shoreline, narrow your search to an eighth of a mile. You must eliminate water to successfully bag spring flounder.

The first step I take while eliminating water on a strange ecosystem is to look for a shoreline that has stands of roseau cane. Roseau has an intricate root system somewhat like a smaller version of mangrove, and it gives baitfishes a place to linger, hide, and dodge larger predators. It is best to fish these areas during the first couple of hours of a falling tide. As the water recedes, baitfishes must leave the cover and the predator/prey dynamic begins. Roseau cane is common in most bay systems, but it is especially common on Sabine Lake, Calcasieu, and along the Louisiana coastline. The Galveston Bay complex has some good stands of it as well, especially in East Galveston Bay and the lower part of Trinity Bay along the Anahuac Refuge shoreline.

Oyster reefs are unique ecosystems. In open, barren bay systems, they are oases in the desert. They are great spots for small baitfishes to seek refuge and feed on microorganisms. This in turn makes them great places to contact opportunistic predators. Reefs harbor your typical batfishes like mullet, menhaden, glass minnows, and crab, but they also draw some unusual species. Sand eels are one of the most prolific bait species found on oyster reefs and a favorite prey item. This is especially true during April, when the menhaden are small and shrimp are hard to find. It is a rare occurrence to catch an oyster reef flounder during this time that does not have a sand eel or two in its belly. This should be a cue to anglers.

James France, former owner of Catch-Em Lures, said a good way to catch these eel-loving flatties is to fish with the Sabine Snake: "We produced the Sabine Snake specifically for reefs. Sometimes, when they get to feeding on the eels, they do not want anything else. That's when the Snake becomes a real go-to bait."

Indeed, the Sabine Snake can be a go-to bait. I have fished on reefs numerous times and had great success with the firetiger and junebug colors. The lure has incredible action and successfully mimics the herky-jerky movements of a sand eel.

The Norton Sand Eel is another good choice. This bait has come on strong in the last few years, and comes in a variety of colors for various water conditions and personal preferences.

During drought years, cutlass fish, also known as ribbonfish, are common on oyster reefs and flounder will absolutely gorge themselves on them. Good cutlassfish imitations include the Bass Assassin, Slug-go, and Mr. Twister Slimy Slug, which is a favorite choice of Matagorda Bay guide Capt. Don Wood. Matagorda, by the way, has some first-class oyster reefs.

The most important thing to keep in mind about any of these lures is to fish them on a heavy jighead. Fishing with 1/8- and 1/4-ounce jig heads may give the lure a more life-like appearance, but you need something that will get down to the bottom and fight heavy spring currents. I go with at least a 3/8-ounce jighead, but actually prefer a 1/2-ounce. Remember, you cannot catch fish unless they can see or hear the lure.

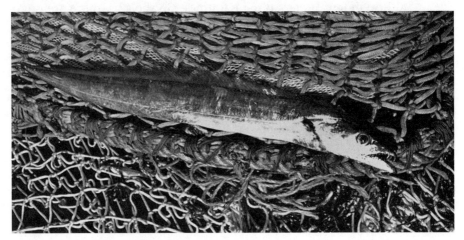

Cutlass fish, aka the ribbonfish

Drift with the current and let the lure bounce, bump, and crash into the oyster reef. Water conditions during spring usually range from off-colored to murky to just plain nasty, so anything that might grab attention is worth trying.

Make sure you have out enough line so you are not vertically fishing. The lure will not work properly that way. In addition, it is important to keep contact with the lure. Springtime game fish are not overly aggressive and often hit soft plastic lures very lightly. Use a super sensitive monofilament or braided line for best results.

Keep in mind that all oyster reefs are equal, and not all parts of an oyster reef are the same. It is important to look for the structure within structure. An oyster reef is a structure all by itself, but there is structure on top of that structure. A big clump of oysters rising up on a slight ridge on a reef with an average depth of 10 feet is structure on structure. A sunken boat on a reef is structure on structure.

Spring & Summer Surf Flounder

Although few anglers pursue flounder in the surf, there are quite a few of them there. The typical drill for flounder is to stay out in deeper water during low tides and move into the shallows when it is high. That is actually quite typical of all predatory species, but for flounder, it is especially true.

It is very difficult to find big schools of flounder in the surf. The fish usually scatter out, but there are places to look for them. To a novice, a stretch of surf looks like any other, but to the experienced angler, there are dramatic differences and certain "structure" to consider, such as points.

Points are parts of the shore that extend into the water, and they can be small or quite large. The most common configuration extends out at right angles to the beach. Occasionally, the beach will turn and a "point" will look more like a "bend," but they are essentially the same. Smaller points are less noticeable, but still detectable by the current rips they produce, or by the way the breaking waves crash on them.

Most anglers choose to fish at the tip of the point because that is where the most baitfishes congregate, and thus predators show up. Going back to the beach, the sides of a sandy point are good, especially in the "pocket"— a depression scooped out of the beach by crashing waves and current.

Bowls are another type of surf structure. Bowls typically indent into the shore and form between two points. Many bowls form in what surf anglers call a "teacup" configuration. If you ever hear someone saying they caught fish in the teacup, they are not speaking in code but prob-

Fish points in the surf where baitfish congregate.

ably talking about a bowl in the surf. Some bowls are subtler and you can only see them when tides are low, which brings up another point. During winter months, when low tides are common after northers lash the stretch of surf you fish, bring a GPS and camera. Photograph the structure and mark its location with the GPS. This will give you a huge advantage over other anglers who spend less time preparing, and help you eliminate a lot of surf when the fish are biting.

Fishing a bowl involves working along the edges and paying special attention to the upper rims or spots where the bowl makes a transition to a point. The center of a bowl can be great, too, because these are often the deepest points, and in shallow surf, sudden depth usually means fish.

Troughs or "guts" are the long depressions or ditches running parallel to the shoreline and sandbars. Surf anglers often talk about fishing "between the sandbars," which refers to fishing the troughs. The sandbars can be the bottom between the troughs, or an actual "bar" formed by current. Bars often parallel the shore for great distances. When surf-fishing for flounder, concentrate on the inner bars. Most surf-fishing experts agree that fish feed along the outer, sloping front-side of the bar. They gravitate toward the bottom where the sloping front of the bar ends.

Learning to identify this "surf structure" will go a long way toward fishing the surf without much guesswork.

If a beach has rock jetties, wrecks, or old pier pilings on it, concentrate some of your efforts there (see pic below). Beachfront flounder like to bond to structure, and on beaches, there usually is not much structure. One fine exception is Constance Beach south of Hackberry, Louisiana. The government has constructed a rock jetty system consist-

ing of large granite piles stacked 100 yards from one another parallel to the beach. They designed this to control beach erosion, but it has greatly enhanced the fishing in the area. I know of a couple of anglers who routinely hop from pile to pile and collect impressive stringers of flatfish. The beachfronts in Galveston and Corpus Christi have small rock jetties that will hold surprising numbers of flounder as well.

FLOUNDER ON THE PLANKS

Piers can be good spots to intercept flounder. Where to position oneself on a pier is a tough call because the flounder could be anywhere. In my experience, it is best to arrive early and set up close to where the veteran pier anglers set up. They usually know the best areas. Tide tables are also important to watch. A super high tide will push the flounder closer to shore, while a low tide will have them out deeper. This is just common sense when you get down to it.

Pier fishing can get confusing and hectic when the trout are running because outdoor writers like me put out good reports and the public responds by packing the pier. Be prepared to fish arm to arm with other anglers when the fishing is good.

With this in mind, I have come up with a checklist of items and skills a newcomer to pier fishing might need. These are the basics and a few other things I consider essential; you should know to bring a rod, reel, hooks, etc.

- Get a tide chart and read the relevant chapter in this book. Start fishing before the high tide. High tides typically peak when there is a full or new moon.
- Be patient and stick with your spot. When the fish are not around the pier, there is nothing you can do about it.
- Learn how to tie good knots. Lifting a fish onto a pier with a weak knot is a surefire way to lose it.
- If fishing with live bait, bring a good bait bucket. Strong, lively bait will out-fish weak stuff every time.
- Bring pliers because you will catch hardhead catfish; a good stick to whack them in the head with would not be a bad idea, either.

SUMMER STRATEGIES

Many misinformed anglers have the idea that when the water temperature reaches beyond the mid 70s, flounder leave the marshy cuts for the main body of a bay system. Some of them probably do, which accounts for the increasing number of small flounder found along bulkheads and shell pads during summer months, but most flounder stay very close to the places they first inhabit when entering a bay system; they might actually come to the same places year after year.

In the mid 1990s, Sabine Lake guide Capt. Skip James, initiated a tagging and radio telemetry study of flounder on his home body of water. He tagged hundreds of flounder and divided them into zones. Yellow tags were for one area, blue for another, and red for the final zone. What he found was that flounder did not trade much between zones on Sabine Lake: "After several years of research, we found that flounder were basically territorial once they moved into a bay system. There was not a whole lot of moving from one cut to another or one drainage to another. Once the fish we tagged move in during the spring, they didn't start moving out until fall."

Captain Skip James

In 1996, James and I began an ongoing tagging program with the kind help of Strike King, who graciously provided us with FinPals tagging equipment. In April 1997, Reverend Jim Darnell and his wife Beth, who produce the syndicated television show *God's Great Outdoors*, came to fish Sabine Lake with me. In the course of the show, we tagged several floun-der. Three months later,

Mike Denman of Orange caught one of those flounder in the exact same cut where Darnell and I tagged it. After talking to Denman, I learned he actually caught the fish on the exact point where we landed it the first time. This very rewarding experience convinced me at least some flounder are very territorial, which allowed me to adapt my fishing techniques and conservation efforts in a more intelligent way.

Still, summer does not seem like the right time to catch flounder. Most anglers imagine flounder fishing comes with falling leaves and high school football season. To a lesser extent during the last few years, more anglers have come to realize that spring provides excellent fishing opportunities for flatfish. However, summer flounder fishing is a mystery to many anglers, and although it is not as consistent as spring or fall, summer can give up plenty of flounder for those who know where to look.

To consistently bag good numbers of quality-sized flounder during summer, concentrate on the wider and deeper parts of cuts in a bay system. The largest concentrations of flounder are usually in the first 1/8-mile of these cuts during the dog days of summer because they have more tidal water exchange on each tidal movement, which keeps these areas somewhat cooler than the shallow backwater. I am not saying these areas hold any more flounder than other cuts, but I have caught more in them than in other locations on bay systems in summer, so that's where I go. Cooler water temperatures usually mean a higher content of dissolved oxygen, which benefits flounder two-fold. First, it obviously gives them more oxygen, which they need to be effective predators, and secondly, it attracts more baitfishes. Scientists have learned that one of the reasons certain fish species in bay systems do not feed as aggressively during summer as they do in spring and fall is decreased levels of dissolved oxygen.

I have always had far more success on incoming tides during

summer months. In fact, I usually check the tide charts and mark off the days with the highest tides to concentrate on them. When these tides are running high, seek flounder along the main shorelines of bay systems.

Since flounder body up in groups ranging from a few individuals to several dozen, it is best to utilize pattern casting. This means to try to cover every square inch of key flounder habitat in a given area. Throw to a spot and then throw a foot or two past with your next cast until you have covered the entire area. It often pays to work the same spots over twice, since you might miss the exact spot by a few inches. Since flounder are not very mobile, the key to catching them is to cover lots of ground.

Summer is a time of high barometric pressure and I believe this might have something to do with the slowdown in flounder fishing, particularly during late July and early August. Think about it: Have you ever wondered what makes fish decide to bite or stop biting on a perfectly beautiful, calm day in summer? It is very frustrating knowing that fish are in a specific location, but refuse to bite. I am talking about the times when a normally hot area does not give up a single strike. There are days when the best-planned strategy just does not seem to click. Either the fish are trying to get some sort of revenge on the anglers, or unseen factors are at play. Some of these unseen factors receive strong documentation by scientists while others will likely forever remain mysterious.

Barometric pressure can be an important part of the fish biting equation, but it is greatly misunderstood. Barometric pressure is the force of the atmosphere usually expressed in terms of the height of a column of mercury in an instrument (barometer) used for measuring atmospheric pressure. While trying to reach equilibrium, the air on top compresses the air that is lower, or closer to Earth. The compression of air caused by high pressure causes heating of the molecules. This heating raises the temperature of the water in the air, causing it to evaporate. On the other hand, in low-pressure areas, the air closer to Earth becomes uncompressed and allows the air to cool. At this point, the air temperature drops and allows the water in the air to fall below the saturation point, causing clouds to form. High pressure usually means few clouds and calm winds. Low pressure can spawn strong gusts and rain.

According to fish biologist Dr. Gary Van Gelder, by applying basic math it is easy to see that small changes in barometric pressure probably have little affect on fish directly. A pressure change from 30 inches of mercury to 29 inches represents a pressure change of only 13 inches of water: "In this situation, a fish would have to move one foot deeper to maintain the exact same pressure on its body."

On the other hand, there may very well be something to falling and rising barometric pressure, as this signals major changes in sky conditions, wind direction, and so on. According to Van Gelder, there are two explanations that have at least some validity in explaining why fishing is sometimes more difficult on "bluebird" days such as those that follow a major cold or storm front: "One explanation based on observations made by scuba divers and that's consistent with my fishing experience is that there is an active feeding period as the cold front moves into an area. The theory is that the fish gorge and are less active during the post-front bluebird sky period. The second explanation is that the higher levels of ultraviolet radiation adversely impact the smaller life forms in the food chain, and infrared radiation associated with sunlight under very clear sky conditions. It's possible the bigger fish have learned that feeding success is lower during these periods, and thus maintain a lower level of activity until the food chain gets active and becomes more readily available."

Many anglers seem to prefer the pressure to be around 30.00. Many professional fishing guides feel this is the peak biting period and say anything higher turns the bite off. There might be some science to back this up. Recently, the Florida Game and Fish Commission put several species of saltwater fish in a large observation tank with a controlled atmosphere to study how pressure would affect their feeding habits. Between 30.00 and 30.10 barometric pressure, the fish started to feed. When they turned the pressure up to 31.30, the fish died. The scientists believed the confined tank did not allow the fish enough depth to equalize the pressure on their bodies.

Since discovering this information, I have often asked myself if this is the reason fish shut off on dead calm days. I like high pressure for Gulf fishing because it calms the seas, but when the barometer gets too high, I have found fish do not cooperate. Now I know why.

Studies have shown that barometric pressure can slightly alter the size of blood vessels. During times of high pressure, there is more physical pressure on blood vessels, constricting the expansion of the vessel wall. Conversely, during times of low barometric pressure, there is less pressure on blood vessels, allowing the vessel wall to expand. In humans, these changes could cause migraine headaches, and it is possible that fish also face discomfort under pressure.

With that said, it might pay you to be mindful of the barometric pressure while fishing. I started keeping a very detailed log of my fishing activities, and make notes of changes in the barometer in relation to fish biting patterns. I hope this will shed light on the little mysteries that pop up regarding fish behavior. I hope to link this to the bite patterns at some of my favorite fishing holes across the coast.

THE FABULOUS FALL RUN

Come time for high school football and falling leaves, mud minnows become a hot commodity in coastal communities. So do certain types of soft plastic baitfish imitations. Whitetail deer and redfish grab most of the headlines, but to a dedicated and growing core of Texas anglers, fall means flounder fishing.

Starting with the first strong cold fronts and the change of the daily photoperiod, a massive number of flounder begin funneling from bay systems, through river channels and passes, and into the Gulf of Mexico. Outdoor writers and anglers dub this mass migration the "fall flounder run," and for dedicated flatfish aficionados, it is a sacred time to be on the water. More flounder are actively moving and feeding than during any other season.

In the early to middle part of fall, go back to the marshy cuts to find flounder. The difference between fall and spring is that flounder are usually concentrated more heavily this time of year. When you find one flounder, you are liable to find a whole bunch more.

I have had more success in the fall by spending little time in the interior of cuts and concentrating on the first 30 yards, then working 100 yards or so into the cut. This is especially effective after big northers, when baitfishes are seemingly pouring out of the marsh.

If there is a flat adjacent to a cut or pass leading out of a bay system, make sure and spend plenty of time working it over. Flounder are suckers for shallow flats in fall, especially during morning hours because they congregate to soak up the warm water. (Shallow flats warm quicker than other spots.)

As the run begins to fizzle, look to jetty systems and passes leading into the Gulf for the hottest action. Flounder cannot move great distances in a short time, so many times when the flounder have left the bay they will body up at jetties on their way to spawn. Jetty fishing for flounder is much like fishing in the bays, but with different terrain. The key is to look for lots of baitfish and the spots where eddies form and tidal exchange is strong. Keeping in mind that jetties extend southward into the Gulf, a good place to look for flounder is at the southern tip. These areas are important to cover because there are usually major eddies, and like in a marshy cut, these eddies hold heavy concentrations of small baitfishes, which in turn draw flounder.

Sometimes these eddies can be huge. At the Galveston jetties I have seen eddies 80 yards across, and at the Sabine jetties, they are commonly 40 to 50 yards across. To narrow down your search, use electronics to find the current washout, which is usually just beyond the last hunks of granite.

Another good spot to look for flounder at jetties is in the boat cuts. The tidal exchange can be extreme and flounder can be thick, but they are often difficult to fish because of heavy current and boat traffic. The easiest place to position is to the side of the cut, where it is possible to throw against the current and allow the bait to drift backwards.

Fishing the passes between a bay and the Gulf north of a jetty system can be equally productive. The key here is to understand points of migration. A "pass" does not necessarily have to mean a bottleneck area like Sabine or Rollover Pass. A "pass" can also be an historic area of flounder migration. Sea Wolf Park in Galveston Bay is a fine example. Every fall, hundreds of flounder end up in ice chests here as they pass through the bay toward Gulf waters. There is no physical reason the flounder have to move through this spot, but they are there every year. It's part of their historic migration route.

There is another location like this on the Intracoastal Waterway near Sabine Lake. There is no reason the flounder have to move through this particular area, and in fact, it seems as if they go through quite a bit of trouble to do so. I have started calling these locations "Genetic Migration Points." I believe these fish have become genetically programmed to move through these locations. Perhaps eons ago, they first started migrating through these spots because some structure forced them to, and their ancestors simply travel the same route through some kind of genetic encoding far too strange and complex for me to understand.

The reason I mention these locations is that if you can find one similar, you may very well have your own hotspot that no one else would fish. I found one in the spring of 2002 when I stopped to ask a couple fishing from the side of the road what they were catching. I expected to hear croaker and maybe a few redfish, as it was in the ship channel away from any cut or bay. They held up a stringer of flounder. This was during the last part of the spring migration. The next day, I showed up there and caught a limit. The bite lasted about a week and then they were gone. Around the same time in 2003, they showed up again and the same pattern followed.

My best guess is those fish were headed up toward Bessie Heights Marsh in the Neches River. Whatever the case, it convinced me there are some spots these fish move through and, more importantly, hang around during certain times. A bass fisherman would call these spots "staging points," and I guess that is what they are. Perhaps the fish stop there to rest and eat, or just simply stop for no discernable reason.

I have put together a map of the Sabine area marking these genetic migration points I have gathered myself and by asking around. Some of them are strange, while others make perfect sense. Still, as long as they help you catch more fish, it does not really matter. I am all about trying new things, and in this situation, it is unorthodox but highly effective.

WINTER FLOUNDER

Most flounder leave the bays in fall, but a fair number hang around in the bays for some reason. It might seem strange, but I believe the key to locating flounder in winter is to find the trout. Therefore, winter flounder fishing is, perforce, a study in winter trout fishing.

I love to catch big speckled trout, but the methods involved in going after true trophy specimens are difficult, mentally strenuous, and physically taxing. I passionately crave catching big sow trout, but dread the methods I choose to employ. Catching these prized specimens goes against most of my other coastal fishing principles. Forget about covering lots of water, "walking the dog" with a topwater plug, and catching lots of fish. Generally speaking, wintertime trout fishing is the polar opposite.

Nonetheless, wintertime offers the best chance to score on huge trout, the kind that make dreams and taxidermists a living. If we choose to pursue these yellow-mouthed beauties during the coldest months of the year, we must be willing to go the extra mile to get the job done. The task is daunting, but the rewards can be life enhancing.

Do not plan on seeking winter trout as you would during spring or fall when the fish are showing obvious signs of feeding and easy to locate. There will not be any birds or boats circling an area to give you hints. If you want to get the job done when the water temperatures are inhospitable, planning is essential.

Keith Comeaux of Biloxi, Mississippi, is a diehard winter fisherman. He recommended mapping out a couple of good areas and sticking to them: "The first thing to keep in mind is that you're not going to get many bites, so don't expect it. My rule is that I wade an area for 90 minutes. If I do not get a bite by then, I hit another area and work it for 90 minutes. Usually by this point, though, I can find some action."

Comeaux, who fishes from the Chandeleur Islands to Galveston Bay, fishes two types of locations almost exclusively: "I target mud flats near deep water, and oyster reefs. The mud flats are tough to wade, but hold more big trout than any other area in winter. The trout hole up in the deep water and come out to the shallows to feed when the mud flats warm up. A muddy, black bottom helps to hold in heat, so the water temperature will be a few degrees warmer than the surrounding deep areas. The oyster reefs also hold some big fish, but I catch them there less frequently. I think they're simply drawn to the baitfish there."

His strategy involving mud flats near deep water mirror my wintertime trout tactics. Frankly, I consider the Intracoastal Canal and other commercial ship channels a trout angler's greatest ally during the cold months. As Comeaux said, black mud bottoms in shallow water retain heat on sunny days, and by the afternoon, the water temperature may be as much as 10 degrees warmer than surrounding deep water.

It is advisable to wade these areas mainly in the afternoons on a high tide. By midday, the water temperature has had a chance to rise and the high tides will ensure there is enough water on the flats.

Manmade islands show up in many spots along the Intracoastal Waterway and they can be used to your advantage; the Intracoastal on many bay systems cuts through the north end of the bay. Some of the best water for wading will be the north shoreline. That is because prevailing winds this time of year will be from the north and the water around the north shoreline will be flat water. While the north shoreline may provide protection from the wind, you can find plenty of action on the south end of the ecosystem. Windward shorelines are often where baitfishes and big specks pile up.

Speaking of bait, it is important not to fret over a lack of bait activity. In the fall or summer, bait activity worth fishing might be an acre raft of menhaden or a big school of shrimp. In the winter, you simply will not find many large congregations of bait. Instead, look for something as simple as a few mullet swimming around.

You might be scratching your head, still wondering why I explained so much about winter trout fishing. Very few anglers know anything about winter flounder, but plenty know about winter trout—and the two species hang in the same areas.

Trout hang in deep water during cold periods of low tide and then move onto the flats on warm days to feed. Flounder that hang around in the bays do the exact same thing. You can literally follow the strong trout feeding and catch good numbers of flounder. It may seem strange, but it is true.

Slow-sinkers are the most effective and widely used wintertime trout lures, and they work great for flounder, too. They appeal to the slow metabolism of cold-blooded fish, which can be quite lethargic during winter months. Much of the lures' popularity can be attributed to the fact that the Texas state record trout was caught on a super-slow-sinking Corky. The hottest slow-sinker on the market now is MirrOlure's Catch 2000, a hard plastic bait that sinks like the Corky but can withstand more than a few strikes by toothy trout or rogue redfish.

"Since it came out, I would have to say the Catch 2000 has remained one of the hot sellers and best big trout producers on the market," said James "Tally" Taliaferro of Tally's Tackle in Groves, Texas. "It has a lot of the same appeal as the Top Dog by its appearance, but it fits the application of some of the soft plastic lures."

Tally introduced me to the lure when it first came out, and I have been impressed with its ability to catch fish and its genuine slow-sinking action; I have caught some nice flounder on it. The only difference in the way I fish a Catch 2000 or Corky for flounder versus speckled trout is I allow the lure to actually hit bottom and then slowly drag it a couple of feet, pause, and move it again.

Finding big concentrations of flounder or any predator species is tough in winter. Fish are cold-blooded and do not really like winter. If they can find sanctuary from winter weather, they tend to do so, which is why warm-water outfall canals are such great fishing holes.

Along the Texas coast, there are several warm-water discharges from energy plants and refineries that can harbor incredible numbers of fish and, quite often, the best bay fishing winter has to offer.

I grew up fishing around the Entergy Plant near Bridge City. It is like several similar outfits along the coast in that it cools its turbines by pumping water from one canal and expelling it into another. In this case, the water is coming from a marsh bordering the Lower Neches Wildlife Management Area and is exiting into a canal that leads to the mouth of the Neches River. Both usually hold salty water during winter.

Baitfishes congregate in such warm waters during cold spells, making a sort of buffet for a host of flounder that winter in the bays. They are great for human predators, too, since the cold-blooded fish become much more active feeders in these spots than in much colder surrounding waters.

Warm-water discharges come in many forms. They can be a huge cooling plant that spews out thousands of gallons of warm water a minute, or a small drainage pipe or culvert with light flow. Chemical refineries often have small pump stations that produce warm-water flow that divert into underwater pipes. Any of these areas can hold a surprising number of fish. However, it is safe to say the more flow and the warmer the water compared to the surrounding waters, the more fish there will be.

Flounder often sit downcurrent and can be found in eddies that form near drop-offs. Small baitfishes cannot negotiate current very well, so they often get stuck in eddies. Flounder will stack up in these eddies and gulp up the shad, shrimp, and whatever else ends up there.

Something to keep in mind is that even small flows from a single drainpipe can draw fish. They may not hold massive schools, but even a slight change for the positive in water temperature can make a difference in cold weather. It is very important to look for the little things in these spots, since very often that is all it takes to attract game fish.

Galveston area guide Capt. Guy Schultz said the Houston Light and Power (HL&P) outfall in Trinity Bay is a great warm-water spot: "Everyone in our area has heard the stories of guys filling up boatfuls of fish in that area before limits were put in place, and I don't doubt those stories have a lot of truth to them. Sometimes, catching fish in these areas is like shooting fish in a barrel. It's up to the angler to abide by limits and do the right thing."

I agree 100 percent. Situations where fish are stacked in a particular area may make it tempting to go over the limit just a little—or sometimes a lot. It is important to realize other anglers use these spots, too, and just a few anglers keeping too many fish can have an impact on the resource. If we all stay legal, these wintertime hotspots should stay productive for many years to come, and that will make all of us happy.

Chapter Nine

Texas-sized flounder tactics

Two elderly gentlemen had anchored at a spot in the ship channel near Southwest Louisiana's Lake Calcasieu. From their appearance alone, I could tell they were veterans of coastal angling. Their leathery skin appeared deeply tanned from many days spent outdoors. They wore well-worn white rubber shrimping boots and had a look on their faces that said, "Experience is everything." These were not the kind of people you see at a Southern Kingfish Association tournament or at a Safari Club International fund-raiser. These men were simply diehard, lifelong anglers, which are the kind I most like study.

"You men catching anything?" I asked while slowly cruising past their boat.

At first, they did not say anything, but the man in the back of the boat nodded at the one in the front and he slowly raised a chain stringer from the water. In my entire life, I have never seen such a large stringer of flounder. There were nine of them and the smallest was probably 4 pounds with the largest topping out at about 8 in my best estimation. I probably drooled enough to chum king mackerel from the rigs 10 miles away.

"You catch any of those here?" I asked.

"Well, we caught them all in the ship channel using mullet," one of the men said.

At this point, he pulled an 8-inch mullet out of the bait basket and showed it to me.

"Son, you remember this and remember it well. If you want to catch big flounder, then you've got to fish with big bait and you've got to fish deep."

He then motioned for me to move along. I guess sharing that information was as generous as he was going to get that day. I was flabbergasted and have not shared that encounter in print until now. Since then, those words etched themselves in my memory and have spawned a deep passion to aspire to match the mighty catch I saw that day.

After conducting much research, both in the scientific community and from veteran anglers, I have come to the following conclusion: The gentlemen in the boat were right. If an angler wants to catch "trophy" flounder, then fishing with large bait in deep water is the way to go.

Sure, fishing marshy cuts and shorelines is effective. I have written about them dozens of times because they are the ultimate way to catch numbers of legal-sized flounder. Purposely pursuing the big ones, though, means trying some different methods, including fishing structure related to deep water. How deep? An angler fishing for snapper in 200 feet of water in the Gulf of Mexico broke the state record for flounder in Mississippi. That is an extreme example, but it validates what scientists have said for many years: big flounder prefer deeper water than small and medium-sized ones do.

SHIP CHANNELS

The section of ship channel between a bay system and the Gulf is where many of the largest flounder will be. Shrimpers who have dragged these areas can validate this by the amount of big flounder by-catch that ends up in their nets.

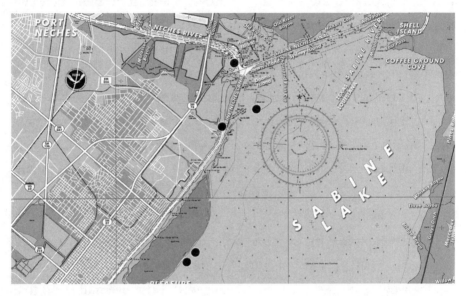

Sabine-Neches ship channel map

Robert Vail, an Upper Texas Coast fishing guide, said years ago when he used to run trawls in the Sabine-Neches ship channel just south of the Causeway Bridge at Pleasure Island, catching lots of big flounder was not unusual. In fact, it was commonplace: "We used to get some huge flounder in the trawls, and the shrimpers still get some real big ones from time to time."

Targeting these deep-water flatfish requires electronics because there are no visual markers to go by. Underwater, however, there are plenty of signs that point to possible flounder "holds" or areas where they congregate.

"The ideal hold is a small spot or shelf on the edge of a steep drop-off," Vail told me. "This hold might be a 20-square-foot area in 15 feet of water that borders a 30-foot drop-off. In most situations, the 15 feet zone would gradually get shallower as you move toward the bank, but then drop off suddenly into the main channel."

Such places provide a zone where flounder can feed on bait-fishes that come to the spot, and it provides a place to trade between the deeper main channel and the shallower shoreline.

Ship channel flounder feed in stages just like those in the cuts and bayous on a bay system. They move up closer to shore to feed, then back toward deeper water, and back again. After locating such a spot, fishing it is the second challenge. Position the boat where the anchor is right on the edge of the hold so you can fish straight up and down. For tackle, although I usually recommend a good spinning combo for floun-der fishing, in this situation a stout casting rod spooled with braided or fusion line works better.

The terminal rig is simple because it consists of only a 1-1/2- or 2-ounce jighead. This may require visiting a top-end tackle store, but it will be well worth the effort. On this jighead, I use live mullet up to 8 inches long or some of the larger croaker you can buy from a bait camp. There are very few small flounder in these spots, so do not be afraid to use a big bait. I once saw a 3-pound flounder hooked on a foot-long mullet that my fishing partner and I were using for alligator gar bait (*see photo on facing page*).

Once you have baited the jighead, simply lower it down over the spot, sink it to the bottom, and start jigging up and down. If flounder are there, they usually hit pretty fast, so if you do not get a bite within 10 minutes, move elsewhere.

If you are having a hard time finding holds, you can achieve pos-itive results by positioning the boat on the edge of the drop-off and

using the same technique. If you have a trolling motor, set it on low and let the bait drag the bottom. If you do not, then make long casts parallel to the drop-off so you can cover more ground.

There are shallows along ship channels, and flounder certainly move to these spots to feed. I have found that many of the big ones simply stay deep, but you can certainly catch some saddle blankets in the shallows as well. The key is figuring out which spots are best. Once you start looking for holds, that is quite easy, but narrowing down shallow banks in the ship channel can be tough. It might seem as easy as moving toward the shallows from the deep hold, but that is not always the case. Look for little points coming off the shoreline—I am talking about even tiny fingers of soil that extend out toward the deep—and concentrate on them. These ship channel flounder usually congregate around structure, even more so than their bay-dwelling counterparts, so any structure in the channel is good.

Also, look for any exchange of water, whether it is a cut, pipe, or space between islands. Water exchanges are places flounder can easily intercept baitfishes, and no matter where they are, flounder like it easy. Remember, flounder are lazy fish, and if you use these tactics, you can locate not only the lazy ones, but the big, fat ones as well.

Oyster Reefs in Spring

Other areas that can be full of big flounder include the vast oyster reefs that cover much of our bay systems. Fishing here involves a very different method than in ship channels or jetty areas. Since many oyster reefs have pretty much the same depth throughout, drifting while fishing a bait on the bottom is the prime way to locate flounder.

This method is all about the terminal rig, what I call a "breakaway rig." Its originators designed it to allow the angler to break off the weight without losing the entire rig. I detailed this rig in the Seasonal Patterns chapter, but it deserves mention here because I use a slightly different version for big flounder.

To make a breakaway rig, attach a barrel swivel to a 24-inch, 10-pound-test monofilament leader. Connect a 1-ounce round weight on one end, and an 18-inch, 25-pound-test shock leader fitted with a treble on the other.

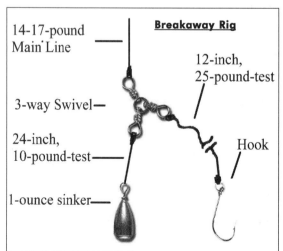

14-17-pound Main Line
Breakaway Rig
12-inch, 25-pound-test
3-way Swivel
24-inch, 10-pound-test
Hook
1-ounce sinker

Using 25-pound or better line allows you to drift over the oyster bed and break off the weight when you snag up instead of losing the whole thing. The treble hook is useful when baiting with big mullet or croaker; setting the hook on a big flounder while drifting can be tough, so having three hooks makes it easier. I slowly raise and lower my rod tip to give the rig a hopping action.

Also as detailed in the Seasonal Patterns chapter, Little-Lindy Joe, Inc., makes a product that is very beneficial for such flounder fishing applications. The No-Snagg Slip Sinker aids working through "unfishable" waters. Its unique shape allows it to twist itself free from obstructions where other sinkers cannot. I have used with an 18-inch braided leader and a live mud minnow when making big drifts over major reefs, and the shell never snagged me.

Live bait is usually best for reef fishing, but I have also had success with plastics. The Norton Sand Eel in glow or chartreuse is a good one, as are the large DOA shrimp.

DOING IT AT THE JETTIES

Jetties are another deep-water area that frequently holds big flatfish. Since jetties serve as sort of a "flounder funnel" between the bay and Gulf, the action can be hot in early March when the fish start moving into the bays, and serve as a fall hot spot right on through December when the flounder exodus to Gulf breeding grounds is complete.

David Geautreaux of Beaumont fishes for flounder in boat cuts at jetties frequently during this productive period, and said some of the biggest fish come from there: "You'd be surprised at how many flounder can be caught at the jetties if you use the right tactics."

Geautreaux uses live mud minnows and a 1-ounce egg sinker rigged on a swivel attached to a 20-pound monofilament shock leader. He hooks the bait through its lips: "When you fish some of the areas that I fish, you need heavy stuff. There are lots of rocks and stuff in these areas, and I would hate to miss a saddle blanket flounder because I was under-rigged. Don't be afraid to use heavy line. I like to anchor around the boat cut and work a little area over real good. Making a good, long cast and dragging it all the way to the boat is important. I have caught many a flounder right at the boat, which is a spot lots of folks overlook."

Something to keep in mind when fishing around these current-laden cuts is to fish with your bait working against the current. This way you can control the movement of the bait instead of the current doing it for you.

For live bait, stick with heavy line at jetties. I like to use a 20-pound monofilament and a 1/2- to 1-ounce egg sinker rigged on a 30-pound shock leader. Using heavier line reduces tackle loss.

John Cervaza of Brownsville has perfected another method for catching big flounder at jetties. He said at the Port Isabel jetties, the fish hold in the dips and pockets of the rocks where baitfishes hold, and in these spots, it is best to fish with a popping cork rig: "I used to go down to those jetties and fish for sheepshead with a popping cork rig and a piece of shrimp. On just about every trip, I would catch a flounder or two along with the sheepshead, so I started to think about how to catch more flounder."

Cervaza ended up adjusting his rig from a popping cork rigged above a monofilament leader attached to a small treble hook, to a braided line leader and a long-shanked single hook: "I went to the braided line because it has no stretch, and that helps to get a good hookup on the flounder. I went to the long-shanked hook because the flounder will swallow it deep. I hook the bait through the lips to keep it lively."

Cervaza said he adjusts the length of the leader in accordance with depth around the rocks: "Most of the time, I fish right up against the rocks in holds that are about 4 feet deep, so I use a 44-inch leader to keep it right above the bottom."

PUTTING THE FINGER ON POINTS

Do not get the idea that the standard flounder habitat of marshy cuts and shorelines do not harbor big flounder. They do, but the other areas receive far less intelligent fishing pressure than cuts and sloughs, and they may be legitimate untapped hotspots in your bay system.

Veteran flounder specialist and Sabine Lake guide Capt. Skip James advised to look to the main points of a bay to target bigger flounder during fall: "In my experience, the biggest fish start exiting the bay first during the annual fall migration. After a couple of cool snaps, they start to exit the marshes and stage on the big points. In Sabine Lake, many big flounder stack up at East Pass, where you have a river and several major bayous meeting the bay. This is a prime place for flounder to stack up and get fat on baitfishes before they make their exodus into the Gulf."

James suggested beginning a fall morning fishing out away from the big points, and slowly working toward the bank as the sun gets toward the sky: "For some reason, these fish tend to start off deeper and move toward the bank as the day wears on."

James said that anyone's favorite flounder bait will work for this method, but he sticks with a 1/4-ounce white Mister Twister jig tipped with shrimp: "If it ain't broke, don't fix it, if you know what I mean. This combo has proven itself to me time and time again."

Something to consider is that even the smallest points coming out of a marsh can be sort of a staging ground for flounder, so consider those spots you normally would not look at. Any visible structure in the water coming out of the marsh can be loaded with flounder. Simply make a few casts around these spots, and if you do not get a bite soon leave. If you do get bit, you know what to do.

TRAINING THE MIND

For me, the hardest part about seeking trophy flounder is being patient. I have places on the Texas and Louisiana coasts where I am fully confident I can catch 20 to 30 flounder, but that is not the way it goes when you are seeking the giant saddle blankets. It is possible to catch tremendous numbers of fish, but expect a half-dozen fish to be a good day. Those six fish might weigh more than two average-sized Texas or Louisiana limits combined, so the trade-off can be worth the effort. Plus, very few anglers catch trophy-sized flounder, so you can be the envy of your friends.

When trophy fishing, size and quality count more than quantity. That is a tough pill to swallow for somebody like me who wants consistent action, but catching a fish that resembles a small halibut sure makes it go down a little easier.

When the flounder begin biting, you can stick with the tried and true methods or gamble with some of these hardcore, big fish-specific techniques. You will probably catch fish either way, but which would you rather have: a stringer full of eating-sized fish, or something that resembles a manhole cover? It is your choice.

These methods do not produce nearly as many fish as the other techniques outlined in this book. There are big flounder for you to catch, but like in trophy trout fishing, you might go all day without a strike, and then hit the mother lode in a brief frame of time.

But when you do you hit, it will hook you for life.

Chapter
Ten

Flounder hotspots

GALVESTON BAY COMPLEX

The Galveston Bay complex is probably the most consistent pro-
ducer of big flounder on the Texas Coast. Moreover, anglers catch the
majority of them during the peak of the fall flounder season. Boatless
anglers also benefit from East Galveston Bay's bounty by fishing in
Rollover Pass off Highway 87 near Gilchrist.

The spring and fall migrations (although I like the spring fishing
here better) generally dictate the fishing at this popular hotspot. From
late February though early April, each incoming tide brings schools of
flounder through the pass from the Gulf. Anglers armed with live mud
minnows and finger mullet can intercept these fish by working the flats
on the north side of the pass and in the pass itself.

"I'd probably rank Rollover Pass as the No. 1 spot to catch flounder when the flounder start to migrate," said dedicated flounder angler

Kevin Danielson of League City. "Rollover is a big pass, and the flounder leaving that side of the bay come through there in a big way. The key to Rollover is being able to wait out the fish, because sooner or later, they will come, and when they do, watch out, because the action will be hot and heavy."

Danielson ranks the shoreline of Sea Wolf Park as the No. 2 migratory point because it is another natural flounder travel route: "A little known fact about the Sea Wolf area is to not be afraid to fish in the deeper water for flounder. Some of the biggest ones never come up in the shallows and stay deep. If you can fish in the deep holes, you will catch big fish. Don't try to wade out to these holes, though, because the current can quite literally kill you."

Capt. Guy Schultz looks to East Galveston Bay to find flounder throughout the fall. Flounder are gorging themselves for their long journey to the deep waters of the Gulf, and the passes linking the bay to the Gulf offer a constant influx of various forage species: "One of the top spots is the Fat Rat area. Bouncing soft plastics along the bottom on an outgoing tide is a great way to find the flounder at this autumn hotspot. Something to keep in mind, though, is the flounder tend to gather up in larger, more concentrated pods on really strong tides, and spread out more on weak tides. In other words, adjust your fishing accordingly. When you find a few on a really strong tide, mark that spot and keep fishing around it because there will be more there."

Danielson also turns his attention to the upper and eastern reaches of Galveston Bay in the fall: "During fall, the shoreline along the Anahuac National Wildlife Refuge can be just alive with fish. Specks and reds are actively feeding and easy to locate, even for anglers who might not be familiar with the area. However, the flounder fishing there is tremendous, especially along the spots where tiny cuts drain the marsh. Do not let all of the action confuse you, and stick with a proven flounder-producing pattern. This usually pays off."

What he means by sticking with proven producers is to go with patterns that have proved successful year in and year out. He suggested pink or white soft plastic shad and shrimp imitations: "Sometimes, there can be so much action you lose sight of things, but if you stick with your original plan, things will usually work out."

One of the most exciting things going here in the fall is seeing the flounder actively feeding along the shorelines. Anglers wading or fishing with carpeted flat-bottom boats or skiffs should look for aggressive flounder attacking bait against stands of cane and near shallow oyster flats. A way to increase the odds of seeing these fish is to wear polarized sunglasses, which take the glare off the water and allow you to see below the surface much better.

Danielson said in fall, boatless anglers can catch plenty of flounder wading the flats near the Texas City Dike and along the shorelines in Kemah and Clear Lake: "The main thing to watch for is the bait. If you can find the bait, you will find the flounder in those areas in the fall. It is that simple."

For winter flounder fishing, West Galveston Bay is as good a spot as any on the coast. The best attribute is the presence of clear water during the winter. Many anglers believe it harbors the clearest water of any area on the Upper Coast during winter, and that is a good thing.

Veteran Galveston guide Capt. Jim Leavelle said the clear water gives anglers a great visual indicator of where fish might be: "Sometimes, the water in that bay is gin clear, but there are usually patches where it is not so clear or maybe off-colored or just a shade darker than the surrounding water. Those can be great spots to fish, as they often indicate baitfish activity."

Before we go any farther, let us define "baitfish activity." In the fall or summer, baitfish activity worth fishing might be an acre raft of menhaden or a big school of shrimp headed toward the Gulf. In the winter, you simply will not find many large congregations of bait. Instead, look for something as simple as a few small mullet swimming around. Mullet are a great indicator of fish. Find mullet and you are on your way to catching fish. Finding small crabs in an area indicates the presence of flounder, as they feed heavily on them during winter months.

West Galveston Bay's southern shoreline is full of small coves, cuts, and islands that can hold good numbers of fish and give the wade-fishing angler plenty of serious options. Much of the water in the area ranges between 1 and 3 feet deep, so fishing it on low tides after a strong front could be difficult. Flounder do haunt the shallows, but you are not likely to see them flopping around bare mudflats in winter, or any time of year, for that matter.

For all of you fall-only flounder mavens, do not forget to look to the north jetty for the hottest action as the bay starts to fizzle. Flounder cannot move great distances in a short time, so many times when the flounder have left the bay, they will body up at jetties on their way to spawn.

SABINE LAKE

Sabine Lake is probably the all-around best flounder-fishing destination on the Gulf Coast. It produced the Texas state record flounder, a beastly 13-pounder, in 1976 and continues to impress to this day. The eastern shoreline, which is actually in Louisiana, is the best choice with more than 20 cuts that empty more than 100,000 acres of marsh.

"Not very many Louisiana fishermen target Sabine because it is off the beaten path," said Capt. Kent Carlson of Point Pleasant Lodge. "But I'm telling you, the fishing there can be awesome, especially after a nice cold front has blown through in the fall. That really gets the flounder going."

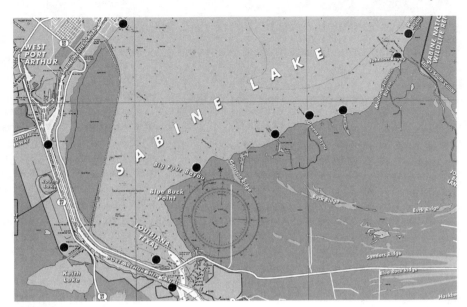

Sabine Lake Hotspot Map

Carlson searches areas that have shallow water with mud or sand banks, and deeper water nearby. Another characteristic that he looks for is areas with a transition from mud to hard bottom: "Anywhere that you can find that kind of bottom just seems to be a magnet for these fish. Once you find a good fishing spot, you should write it down or mark it on a map and be mindful of what the conditions were when you caught them. The fish will return to these areas during the same conditions, as long as the area doesn't go through some drastic change."

Carlson's favorite method for catching these fish is on ultra light spinning tackle. He prefers light, clear monofilament line, and uses small plastic grubs on a 1/4-ounce jighead tipped with a piece of dead shrimp: "Mud minnows are good bait, but I like to use soft plastic grubs with shrimp. I guess it is because you can fish a lot more ground more quickly with a lure, and the shrimp gives a great added attractant."

Sabine Lake flounder expert Capt. Skip James said the Louisiana banks are his go-to spots, but they are certainly not the only option: "One

105

of the best areas can be fished from the bank. It is the revetment wall at Pleasure Island on the north end. For some reason, the baitfish really bunch up at that area, making it kind of a flounder buffet."

The revetment wall stretches for several miles, and while flounder can be caught anywhere along this rocky stretch, James said there are key spots that produce consistently: "There are pipes that trade water from the revetment to the main body of Sabine Lake, and those are by far the best spots to catch flounder there. The Texas Parks & Wildlife Department catches their broodstock for their future flounder-stocking program there. Those spots can be red hot in spring and fall."

Although Keith Lake is not part of Sabine Lake, it is part of the Sabine area ecosystem and deserves mention as a legitimate flounder hotspot. It is the first of a long series of small lakes that border the town of Sabine Pass. The area has many sloughs, cuts, and marshy shorelines with plenty of roseau cane to attract flounder. One of the best spots is where Keith Lake Cut empties into the lake. There is a place where sand meets a mud bottom, and schools of flounder often congregate there. This cut is manmade and has serious tidal pull, which during spring and fall funnels flounder in and out like few other areas. In my experience, the flounder at Keith Lake tend to stack together more tightly than in other areas. In other words, if you catch a flounder in one spot, throw right back there because there is a good chance you will catch another.

For adventurous anglers, Johnson, Fence, and Mud lakes offer a bounty of fishing opportunity at the back end of Keith Lake. The key areas to target are the canals that connect them. Catching flounder moving from one lake to another can be highly productive, and is not something that only happens during spring and fall migration. Any tidal movement can push these flounder through the canals and into your ice chest.

During the bountiful fall season Capt. Daniel Pyle lists wade-fishing as his favorite way of catching fish on the flats near the Sabine-Neches

Ship Channel at the head of Pleasure Island, Stewt's Island, and Sydney Island: "Those areas are perfect for fall fishing because they're all near the mouth of the river that empties hundreds of thousands of acres of marsh. That marsh is full of shrimp, menhaden, and mullet, and will draw in the big predatory fish."

The Louisiana banks offer some tremendous wading opportunities as well, but mostly in small doses. The area from Blue Buck Point to Garrison Ridge is wadeable, but that is about it as far as large stretches of easily wadeable turf go. There are plenty of spots near the cuts on the shoreline to wade, but most are not on maps. It is a trial and error thing.

During winter, most flounder have exited the Sabine ecosystem, but there are some areas that offer a fair to good shot at catching them. One is the mud flats just east of Pleasure Island's north end. I rank it as a real sleeper for serious flounder action. The key here is to fish a clear, warm afternoon on a high tide. The muddy bottom holds heat and will draw in baitfishes from the cooler waters of the nearby Intracoastal, which in turn draws in flounder. High tides are important because low tides, particularly after a strong cold front, leave the area too shallow to navigate. A hidden jewel at this spot is a small oyster reef that you can only find if you are fortunate enough to have GPS coordinates for it, or step on it. This spot is great for flounder year-round.

EAST MATAGORDA BAY

East Matagorda Bay is a real sleeper spot for flounder fishing. The biggest numbers of fish start exiting the bay first during the annual fall migration. However, flounder have what I call a "pre-run" in late August and early September. They are not really running into the Gulf, but start biting better than they did during the mid-summer period. In Matagorda, many big flounder stack up around the Intracoastal

Waterway and the Colorado River. I advise beginning the morning fishing out away from the big points and slowly work toward the bank as the sun gets toward the sky. For some reason, these fish tend to start deeper and move toward the bank as the day wears on.

Matagorda flounder work the shorelines in both spring and fall, so do not overlook them. Key shorelines are those with stands of roseau cane, which you should fish on high tides, as well as those with any kind of cut feeding toward the main body of the bay. You should also not overlook some of the marsh ponds that connect to the main body by only a small cut. One such spot is Boy Scout Lake, which can be loaded with flounder.

Upper Laguna Madre

Upper Laguna Madre is an underrated flounder destination. That is because it is located near Baffin Bay, which for many anglers is the Promised Land of trout fishing. That does not mean Upper Laguna Madre does not offer up some tremendous flounder fishing opportunities.

A surprisingly good method for flounder fishing in the area is to drift the shoreline and fish a live shrimp either free-lined or under an Alameda Rattling Float or Mansfield Mauler. Most of the time this is used for trout, but it can yield quite a few flounder as well.

Many times this area turns on in early June when light southeasterly winds push clear water up from Port Mansfield. With the clear water comes good fishing.

Flounder fishing can be spectacular during fall. The area around the JFK Causeway is unquestionably the best spot when the flatfish are making their migration back toward the Gulf. A live mud minnow or finger mullet slowly dragged across the bottom is a sure way to hang into a saddle blanket.

Whether seeking flounder or any other denizen of Upper

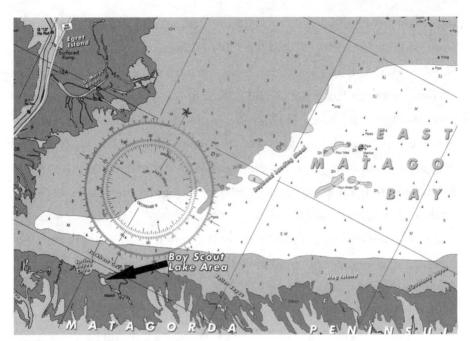

Boy Scout Lake area

Laguna Madre, remember tides. All tidal movements are not equal and deserve special attention for this area. See the Tides chapter for details.

LOUISIANA LOCATIONS

Flounder stocks seem to be holding up well along the Louisiana Coast and providing anglers with some of the most exciting and rewarding fishing action found anywhere.

Constance Beach is one of the most productive but overlooked flounder hotspots. In fact, the flounder fishing is so good at this lonely stretch of shore near the Texas border, a handful of well-informed Texas anglers routinely make the trip over to fill their freezers with tasty flounder fillets. Targeting the fish at Constance Beach is easy. The U.S. Army Corps of Engineers has put large rock piles at various points along the beach to protect the fragile shoreline from water and wind erosion. The rocks serve as great structure for fish and are a virtual magnet for flounder. Look for high tides to provide the best action, and the north and south side of the rocks to hold the most flounder.

Elsewhere on the extreme southwestern coast, the Cameron Ship Channel between Holly Beach and Cameron is as good a flounder fishing spot as any in the state. This is one of the critical migratory spots for flounder, and it tends to get better with each passing cold front. There are only a few good spots to access this location from the bank, and when the fishing gets hot, anglers will line the banks along the sides of the channel while those in boats work the edge of the drop-off. Live mud minnows and finger mullet dragged across the bottom are without a doubt the best baits here, although soft plastics like Twister Tails, chartreuse or white flounder worms fished on a heavy jighead, and Flounder Pounders have gained popularity in recent years.

Other good flounder hotspots in the vicinity include Johnson Bayou Beach and the part of Johnson Bayou near the boat launch at Deep Portage Road.

Veteran flounder angler Kelly Jones of Lake Charles lists Lake Calcasieu as his favorite flounder destination and fishes the refuge shoreline on the eastern side of the lake from the late September until around the week of Halloween: "If you fish the area as much as I do, you start to know what the right and wrong things to do are, what the fish's habits are, and when they move in what areas."

Jones said you can catch these fish at any time during the fall period, but he follows the cycles of the moon to get the best results and to catch the biggest fish: "I've found that during summer, you should follow the moon movements to catch those flounder. Your best fishing is going to be on a full moon or the period around a full moon. That is when the fish bite the best. If you are fishing another moon phase, then there is a chance you will have to work for the fish. On a full moon, catching them is almost a given."

Jones' favorite bait for big flounder is large live mud minnows fished on shallow flats under a plastic bobber. Since he fishes so much, he traps and catches his own bait: "When you flounder fish as much as I do, you have to catch your own bait. Otherwise you could go broke."

Locating the fish at Calcasieu is not that difficult. Jones said to look for cuts that feed the marsh and areas of slack water (eddies) in the cuts: "Something to keep in mind is not to stay in one area too long. If you're not finding fish then you should move on to another spot."

Long time flounder fanatic Ray Patrick said when blue northers do not cause the winds to howl, anglers can collect impressive catches on jigging spoons fished in open water near the famous Mud Lumps out of South Pass. Most of these flounder are quality fish, averaging 1 to 3 pounds: "Once the flounder get to going through this area, you can really catch some impressive numbers. They go into sort of frenzy. I catch them on jigging spoons, which is a little different from the way most fishermen target flounder.

"I have had three men in my boat catch over 100 fish total within a three hours. For fall, you can't beat it."

Patrick said the key to success is finding the big bunches of menhaden and shrimp migrating outward. The flounder are feeding heavily on those that are holding at the structure of the Mud Lumps: "Since we've had a warming trend during the winter lately, the schools of shad tend to be bigger than they were a few years ago. And the flounder are just as hungry."

Patrick recommended using electronics to search for bait in and around the lumps. Once located, mark and fish: "If you want to try this kind of fishing, bring at least eight good buoy markers and mark the spots where you find shad. They're pretty much going to hold to the same spots throughout the morning. Work the area over real good and mark as many spots as you can. This way you can just move over if the spot you're fishing isn't producing."

Many anglers are not familiar with catching flounder on jigging spoons, but it is really quite simple. Fish the spoons in a slow vertical drop around suspended baitfish. Do not get in a big hurry and work your spoon just fast enough to feel it falling. Most of the time, flounder will hit on the fall and all you will see or feel is a slight tightening of the line. This is when you should set the hook.

Patrick uses a Cotton Cordell spoon or Crippled Herring in 3/4-ounce silver or silver with blue back. To maximize fishing time, he recommended making slight adjustments to the lure by removing the treble hook and replacing it with a wide-gapped, thin-wire single hook: "Most spoons come with treble hooks, but they are very difficult to pop off. If you get caught up on one of those lumps of oyster or some other junk that has come out of the pass, you can forget it. Treble hooks are good for the economy, but hard on the angler's pocketbook in these waters."

Capt. Billy Bucano fishes the beautiful marshes around Delacroix Island and said the flounder action there can be tremendous in the fall: "These marshes hold lots of flounder and the angler who watches the tides and movements of baitfish can score in a big way down here."

According to Bucano, variable No. 1 is tidal movement. He believes that tide may be the most crucial element in the flounder fishing mix. He believes the strength of tides can have a dramatic influence on the feeding habits of flounder, especially in major passes: "On the Louisiana Coast, you have lots of passes and they will all hold tremendous numbers of flounder during the fall run. Look for big bayous and passes feeding out into open water to find lots of flounder."

Most anglers in the Delacroix area like to fish with live mud minnows or finger mullet. Since the current in these passes is strong, Bucano fishes with 1- and 1-1/2-ounce egg sinkers rigged on a swivel attached to a 20-pound monofilament shock leader.

Chapter Eleven

A bright future for flounder

A trawl net earns its keep by scraping the floor of the ocean and bay systems. By design, it scoops up everything in its path, including shrimp, the usual intended catch, and many non-target species or "by-catch."

By-catch is a term fisheries managers use to describe unwanted or undersized organisms that shrimpers throw back into the water, dead or dying.

Flounder and other flatfishes are, by design, condensed laterally and spend most of their lives on the bottom. Here they swim on their sides and lie in ambush for unsuspecting baitfishes. The flounder is tailor-made for a simple, sluggish life on the bottom, so it should come as no surprise that among popular sport fishes, flounder rank as the No. 1 victim of bottom trawlers, particularly in the shrimping industry. In fact,

By-catch shrimping

flatfish fans from New England to Texas are pointing to trawling as the chief cause of declining flatfish stocks.

"There's no question that bottom trawling practices have helped to turn what used to be magnificent flounder runs in the spring and fall into nothing more than crap shoot in some areas," said dedicated flatfish angler Gene Breaux of New Orleans, Louisiana. "I used to be a shrimper, so I know how many flounder they catch in those nets. Back in the 1950s, we would catch as many as 300 pounds of flounder in a single pull, and I am not talking about little ones, either. We caught lots of huge fish that recreational fishermen rarely get a chance to see nowadays."

Species-specific by-catch data differs from state to state, but scientists agree that flounder are a large component of by-catch. Texas officials estimate that more than 1.2 million southern flounder die in shrimp trawls annually. Scientists believe that number is even higher in Louisiana, where shrimpers work in shallower water and have greater access to nursery areas frequented by flounder.

"By-catch is a problem that is being talked about quite a bit among fish and game departments, and reducing that by-catch is becoming a big issue among fish and game departments throughout the Gulf and Atlantic states," said Shreveport, Louisiana, attorney and longtime CCA member Fred Miller. "I predict that as more is learned about the effects of by-catch on flatfish and other marine species, we'll see further restrictions on various commercial fisheries."

Miller explained that while by-catch is currently a huge problem, recent innovations have made it something authorities can deal with in a positive fashion: "Conservative estimates show that there are four pounds of by-catch for every pound of shrimp brought in. Just by doing the basic math, you can see that there are many millions of pounds of non-targeted organisms killed in the shrimping industry. But recently, there have been some very promising developments I believe will help everyone from recreational anglers wanting to catch more flatfish to shrimpers who wish to stay in business."

There is real hope on the horizon for not only these popular sport fish, but also the overall health of estuary systems. This "hope" is in by-catch-reducing devices (BRDs).

BRDs have been required of shrimpers operating in the Gulf of Mexico for a few years due to an enormous incidental catch of juvenile red snapper. Now they are required on all commercial shrimping vessels in Texas waters to lessen the killing of flounder and other organisms. Currently, Texas Parks & Wildlife Department (TPWD) biologists are experimenting with several different BRDs to see which ones are best suited for Texas waters.

"We're seeing some real promise in by-catch reduction in shrimp trawls in Texas bays in some of the ongoing experiments being conducted on the Middle Coast," said TPWD biologist Larry McEachron. "Once the details are ironed out, this could be a real boost to Texas coastal conservation efforts."

Officials conducted one-hour comparative trawl tows in Aransas Bay using 32-foot nets during the spring season, and 45-foot nets during the fall season. There were three types of BRDs used: the Fish Eye (FE), Large Mesh Extended Funnel (LMEF), and 2-inch Turtle Extractor Device (TED). According to the study, by-catch varied greatly between seasons and among different types of BRDs, but indicated they have potential for reducing by-catch with limited shrimp loss.

The LMEF had the highest total by-catch reduction in weight and second highest in number with no significant shrimp loss in spring. The TED was first in total by-catch reduction in number during spring, but had significant shrimp loss in weight. The shrimp loss was greater than the total by-catch rate.

Although FE devices have shown by-catch reduction of up to 40 percent in offshore waters and in coastal waters of other states, it had the lowest overall by-catch reduction of the three devices. FE devices did show the greatest reduction in overall by-catch of southern flounder, in both number and weight.

Spot croaker, the most abundant by-catch species, saw the best reduction with the LMEF during spring and fall. During spring, economically important species of management concern had greatest reduction rates with the TED and FE for Atlantic croaker, TED for sandtrout, LMEF for blue crab, and FE for southern flounder.

During fall, Atlantic croaker and sandtrout had the greatest reduction rates in the LMEF, whereas blue crab had the highest in the TED. The FE was the most effective at reducing flounder by-catch.

One thing that concerns TPWD biologists is that by-catch reduction has proven smaller during spring than fall.

"This is a major concern, especially with flounder, because major by-catch organisms are overall smaller in size and found in greater abundance and weight in spring than in fall," McEachron said.

He believes that further development of BRDS for use in bays should go toward reducing smaller by-catch organisms during the spring season, as well as maintaining equal or greater reduction rates during fall with minimal shrimp loss: "There is no doubt that shrimping-related by-catch is going to be a difficult problem to overcome, but there is real promise in the research being conducted now.

"We're currently doing a study in Galveston Bay, and it's possible we could find a viable treatment to this dilemma within the next few years. BRDs are already required on shrimping vessels, and the research we're doing now should be able to help make by-catch reduction not only practical but high effective."

Some shrimpers welcome BRDs because they help reduce overall workload. One shrimper told me: "I've been using them voluntarily for a couple of years. I found out they reduce the number of hardhead catfish in my catch, and that means less pain and agony on these old hands. That alone makes it worth it to me."

Not all shrimpers share that sentiment. One shrimper has put up a website in protest of BRD requirements, especially those targeted

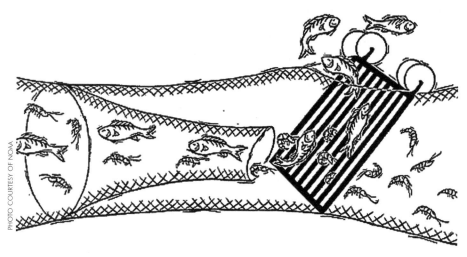

PHOTO COURTESY OF NOAA

BRD illustration

at reducing sea turtle by-catch. On this site, the author claims that in 1989, the first year of mandatory TED use, commercial fishermen produced 430 million pounds of shrimp for consumption in the U.S., and that in 1990, that number fell more than 20 percent. The site also claimed that thousands of small, marginally profitable shrimpers went into bankruptcy, forced to sell their boats and end a way of life that has existed for generations. The site's author claimed: "The only difference between operational characteristics of the 1988 fleet and the 1989 and 1990 fleets were the implementation of TEDs." (sic)

Coastal fisheries officials in Texas have already had to deal with a lawsuit regarding BRDs. Hopefully, whatever judge hears this case will decide in favor of the health of our ecosystems and allow their continued use.

Even a 20 percent reduction in flounder by-catch over the next decade could mean the best flounder fishing Generation X anglers have ever seen. It could also mean a return to the glory days for old salts that yearn for the heavy stringers of yesteryear.

If that makes you happy, there may be even stronger hope for the future of the southern flounder—groundbreaking research by a University of North Carolina, Wilmington (UNCW), scientist.

In 2003, scientists for the first time spawned southern flounder eggs naturally in a controlled environment without hormone induction, and in quantities sufficient for a commercial operation or stocking program. Aquaculturist, Wade O. Watanabe, at the UNCW Center for Marine Science Research said in a report in *Science Daily* that this is another important step toward producing flounder for large-scale fish farming or stocking in the wild: "Our operation shows that you can take wild adult broodstock out of the ocean, and provide the conditions necessary for them to spawn naturally that same year. In the past, for spawning to occur, fish were injected with hormones on a daily basis or implanted with hormone pellets. Now, through natural spawning of recently captured adults, we can minimize the acclimation period for wild-caught fish and the handling-stress on broodfish that would be required if hormones were used to induce spawning."

In the project, funded by the U.S. Department of Agriculture, the National Oceanic and Atmospheric Administration, and North Carolina Sea Grant, Dr. Watanabe set up a brood tank system at the UNCW aquaculture facility in Wrightsville Beach, just east of Wilmington. It consisted of two black cone-shaped tanks, 8 feet in diameter by 4 feet deep, with a volume capacity of 1,250 gallons.

According to the report: "Since scientists believe southern flounder spawn during the winter in December and January, environmental conditions in the brood tanks were manipulated to simulate winter conditions for four and a half months from December through mid-April, 1998. During this period, a group of 24 flounder, weighing from 1-4 pounds and measuring from 14-20 inches long, produced an average of 50,000 fertile eggs per day, enough to satisfy the demands of an aquafarm business."

UNCW Chancellor James R. Leutze said he believed Dr. Watanabe's research has the potential to not only benefit aquaculture, but also help wild flounder populations: "The flounder is a fish that's in trouble. I am remarkably impressed by the creative aspects of Dr. Watanabe's work and its practical benefits to the field of marine science. This research could have a wider impact than any other study in aquaculture."

This could mean a lot to current efforts TPWD scientists are making to spawn flounder in captivity. They are currently working on the project at Sea Center Texas in Lake Jackson with an innovative program called the Texas Gulf Coast Roundup, which is aided by coastal anglers. In this program, TPWD looks to saltwater anglers to target southern flounder and other species during a series of fun and competitive angling events. Participating anglers receive awards for bringing in up to three live specimens from among 20 different popular marine fish, such as red drum, spotted seatrout, and southern flounder.

"We want to make sure we take in the types and sizes of fish that are ideal for hatchery production, research, or educational display needs," said Mike Ray, TPWD director of coastal fisheries field operations. "Flounder are perfect because we are looking to spawn them in captivity, and they are easy to keep alive in a boat's livewell."

At most Roundup events, TPWD officials have put out the word that they want flounder more than most other species. In fact, they have used Roundup procedures to catch their own flounder for the future stocking program.

I got to help when the hatchery truck from Sea Center Texas came to the Sabine Lake area in spring 2002 to gather southern flounder.

"We sent the truck back with more than 60 flounder," said TPWD coastal fisheries biologist Jerry Mambretti. "They would have been happy with as few as 20, but we wanted to make sure they had more than they needed. These fish could go a long way in aiding flounder populations."

We caught most of the flounder at the north revetment on Pleasure Island, but officials also caught some in Keith Lake and in several other areas. My frequent fishing partner Gerald Burleigh and I donated some nice fish we caught on the eastern shoreline of Sabine Lake.

The captive breeding of flounder has been an ongoing struggle for officials at Sea Center and other TPWD hatcheries.

"It's certainly our hope that we can eventually get some kind of stocking program going for southern flounder," former TPWD coastal fisheries director Hal Osburn said at the time of the event. "There seems to be more attention being paid to flounder now than ever, and we want to make sure there's a bright future for this popular species."

Osburn said flounder numbers in Texas have gone on a roller-coaster ride over the last couple of decades. A variety of factors, including by-catch in shrimp trawls and freezes, caused their numbers to decline throughout the 1980s and 1990s.

In 1996, flounder regulations changed in Texas and Louisiana and I hoped this would give the species a much-needed shot in the arm, and it seems to have helped in certain areas, but on the Upper Texas Coast and in parts of Louisiana, fish kills related to oxygen depletion and red tides may have halted the comeback.

"Flounder numbers in Texas certainly aren't bad," Osburn said. "We have many flounder, but they are not at the historical highs of redfish and speckled trout. There are some problems in need of addressing, and that is why we are looking at by-catch reduction, captive breeding, and other issues. We want to make sure the flounder have a bright future."

Osburn's last few years of work at TPWD saw quite a bit of attention paid to flounder numbers, which in the past had rather been neglected. Flounder are the final frontier of inland saltwater fishing. Of the "Big Three" inland species, flounder fall far behind trout and redfish in terms of off-hand angler knowledge and media coverage. Anglers greet the annual flounder migration into our bay systems with great excitement, but it cannot begin to compare to the commotion that surrounds even a fair run of trout or reds.

The reason for this is the fact that flounder engage in no visible schooling activity. A flounder's life revolves on the principles of concealment and ambush, whereas reds and trout gang up and corral schools of baitfishes, thus creating dramatic scenes of predator/prey relations.

Every coastal angler gets excited seeing a school of shrimp doing the "sow speck shuffle," but flounder are a just a tad short on romance for many anglers, and they are somewhat ugly. The public typically needs something pretty and easily understood to rally behind, which is why the original Gulf Coast Conservation Association efforts to restore redfish numbers met with such excitement. Redfish are beautiful and glamorous, but for years, the angling public did not consider flounder as such. I see that changing.

I have written more flounder articles than any other outdoor writer for magazines over the last 10 years, and I daresay more than all Texas writers combined. I am not saying this to brag but to help you understand the level of feedback I get from anglers about the flounder fishery. Literally, every day I get an email about flounder, sometimes multiple ones. Besides how and where to catch them, the No. 1 question I get is: "When is something going to be done to boost their numbers?"

Now, I am happy to report that officials are doing something and I truly believe in the next few years, we will see more focused, determined efforts to restore flounder numbers, and a renewed focus on flatfish at the highest levels. However, this will only happen if you let officials with TPWD and other agencies and organizations—including CCA—know that you want flounder at the top of the agenda. They do not always do what we want them to do, but if they get harassed enough, they will respond, and right now, they are already on the right path; they just need a little prodding from the public.

I know that seeing flounder numbers restored to past levels is plenty to motivate flatfish fanatics to prod, perhaps even harass—and I love it.

How to Fish the Gulf Coast Roundup

Anglers show up at a predetermined location early in the morning to pick up aerated ice chests in which to keep their fish. After signing up, they set out to fish and can turn in their catches to TPWD fisheries biologists from 10 a.m. to 2 p.m.

The events are open to anyone age 21 and older with a valid Texas fishing license and saltwater stamp.

Each participant receives a Texas Gulf Coast Roundup poster and might qualify for additional prizes. TPWD officials award anglers point values for bringing in up to three live specimens.

Participants may register in advance of each event using entry forms available at retail outlets where TPWD officials place Texas Gulf Coast Roundup displays, as well as the event sites.

The Parks and Wildlife Foundation of Texas and Budweiser sponsor the program.

For more information on the Texas Gulf Coast Roundup, visit the TPWD website at www.tpwd.state.tx.us, or call 800-792-1112.

Acknowledgement

Writing thanks for a project like this is always difficult. There are so many people to thank, especially for someone like me who finds inspiration in many places. Still, the following are individuals and institutions that have played a crucial rule in allowing this book to see the light of day.

I would first like to thank God for giving me the opportunity to be able to communicate the wonder of his majestic creation. I often sit in awe of nature and realize it took a serious genius to put this all together. Moreover, the power of prayer has seen me through trying times during the last few years.

Thanks to the brave men and women of the United States military who are shedding their blood so that we have the freedoms we enjoy in this country. Until you have been elsewhere, you really do not know how lucky we have it here. If you want to know who to thank for it, look to the Army, Navy, Air force, Marines, and Coast Guard. They are keeping us free and deserve eternal thanks. To those of you in the military who might be reading this, do not worry about what the mass media is saying. The American public loves you and prays for you daily.

My wife Lisa is the coolest mate a person could have, and puts up with my extreme passion for everything from the outdoors to my Star Wars collection. She and I have been together since our late teens and I cannot imagine sharing life with anyone else. I love you more than you know.

My parents have been there for me through it all and are my biggest fans, so they deserve huge thanks. Actually, words cannot express the thanks they deserve.

Thanks also go out to my band mates in Freak13, plus my life-long friends Chris Villadsen, Patrick Trumble, Lewis Hogan, Shelly Johnston, Clint Starling, Chad Meadows, Reggie Salas, Todd Sonnier, and Todd Jurasek.

Thanks to Hallie Metzger for being a good friend and for sharing your passion for the outdoors. In meeting you, I found a kindred spirit in the pursuit of outdoor thrills. Now, if I could just learn to ride a horse like you do, I would be all right.

Thanks to Kriss Stephens for being there for me and for believing in my work the way you do.

Thanks to Brinke Stevens for her support, and for being a great example of how someone can live their dreams without selling out.

Capt. Skip James has been there for me through thick and thin. He has taught me more about flounder than anyone has, and his sharing of his deep knowledge of the outdoors business is a big part of why I am in this position today. Plus, he makes me laugh more than anyone I have ever met. That is a wonderful thing in itself.

Don Zaidle is more than an editor for me; he is someone I can look to for an honest opinion. In today's world, that is rare, and for it,

I salute him.

Roy and Ardia Neves and *Texas Fish & Game* have been loyal supporters of mine over the years, and I thank them for giving me the opportunity write for their publication.

Duane Hruzek has made sure the public gets a chance to read my books, and he has done a wonderful job getting the message out there. You, my friend, rule.

Thanks to Eric Adams and Manowar for writing music that inspires me to carry on no matter what, and for just being so damn cool—even for a bunch of Yankees.

Thanks to Larry Bozka for giving me a chance quite a few years ago. It was and still is greatly appreciated.

Gerald Burleigh is the only person I know who has followed me into a pit full of rattlesnakes and then one-upped that by getting me in the cage with two 600-pound Siberian tigers. It is hard to find friends like that.

Thanks to all of the fine editors I write for, like Bob West, Roger Cowles, Van Wade, Nick Gilmore, Ted Venker, Robert Macias, Gary Ralston, and Susan Ebert.

Thanks to George Lucas for creating the Star Wars universe. If you do not like Star Wars, you are weird. Sorry, this is a known fact.

Thanks to Stan Lee for creating a huge part of the Marvel Universe. Spider Man, Hulk, Fantastic Four, Daredevil. Need I say more?

Thanks to Stryper for the amazing work you are doing through your music. You truly are the "Soldiers Under Command."

Thanks to Ed Holder for all of his guidance and wisdom over the years.

A special thanks goes out to all of my supporters over the years that have followed my writing and other projects. I am constantly amazed by your support and learn so much from you. I get emails from my readers every day and I always get something out of them, whether it's inspiration or simply a good fishing tip. By far the most passionate ones are the fans of the flounder.

There is no group of fishermen more dedicated, focused, and serious about their favorite species than flounder fans. There is truly a rich tradition with this species that blows me away. It is more than just the tasty fillets or the fact that catching them on a rod and reel is a unique challenge. Flounder are different from other fish in every way, ranging from their appearance to the way they strike a lure.

Those of us who are drawn to this share a bond like no other I have experience in my 12 years of outdoors communications. I am equally at home writing about or fishing for other species, but when I write about flounder, I know I am talking to people who truly care. It is a great responsibility and an honor.

You rule, and all of this is dedicated to you.

In the words of someone much wiser (and richer) than me, "May the Force be with you."

Index